"*Defiant* is a profoundly hopeful and deeply inspirational exploration of the extraordinary women in Exodus as well as the brave, imaginative, justice-seeking, coalition-building, truth-speaking women and girls of today. Nikondeha has given us a great gift to help us through these troubled times."

— DEBBIE BLUE
author of *Consider the Women:
A Provocative Guide to Three Matriarchs of the Bible*

"Grounded in liberation theology, Nikondeha delivers an empowering message of hope, utilizing the twelve women of Exodus and her lived experience in Burundi. Pushing past the patriarchal reading of Scripture, Nikondeha shatters female stereotypes by offering her readers a solid perspective on the labor of women and the role they played as matriarchs in their communities."

— CAROLINA HINOJOSA-CISNEROS
poet, writer, speaker

"Subversive. Collaborative. Glorious. Kelley Nikondeha offers a theological lens for the liberation work women have been part of since ancient times. Now wherever there's an oppressive pharaoh with dehumanizing decrees, let's look for the Nile Network of women collaborating for freedom and justice. Better yet—let's be them."

— IDELETTE MCVICKER
founder of *SheLoves Magazine*

"The story of the exodus is rich but only half-told. Kelley Nikondeha tells the rest of the story through the experiences of the women. Read this and let the exodus come alive in a new way! You will be enriched and the story will develop a power you never expected."

— DOTTIE ESCOBEDO-FRANK
Catalina United Methodist Church

"*Defiant* is exactly how I felt after reading Kelley Nikondeha's book about the subversive women of Exodus. This eye-opening work disrupts the all-too-common habit of skimming over biblical female narratives to get to 'the *real* action' involving men. Finally, the female side of this story gets its due, not as a matter of fairness, but because we need these courageous female role models to embolden women and girls today. *Defiant* combines solid scholarship, creative imagination, current events, a global perspective, and Kelley's own remarkable multicultural story to salvage examples of strong women whose holy defiance, I pray, spreads to God's daughters in today's world, where oppression, abuse, and injustice seem hopelessly entrenched. Let the reader beware: defiance is contagious!"

— CAROLYN CUSTIS JAMES
author of *Finding God in the Margins* and
Half the Church: Recapturing God's Global Vision for Women

"I dare you to read *Defiant* and not be moved to daring. For any woman who has fallen asleep in her own life, Kelley Nikondeha's fierce words, fleshy stories, and fecund imagination will wake her up to the Pharaoh-defying power that is her story, our sisters' story, both ancient and now."

— ERIN S. LANE
author of *Lessons in Belonging
from a Church-Going Commitment Phobe*

"The best storytellers know how to locate the characters that are hidden in plain sight and bring them to center stage. Kelley Nikondeha is such a person. She locates the 'hidden figures' in the book of Exodus—the defiant women—and gives space for their narratives. She masterfully weaves the witness of Exodus women with women of our present era. In the weaving of these stories, Kelley invites us to see what we have failed to see and to listen to the ones whose voices are often overlooked. *Defiant: What the Women of Exodus Teach Us about Freedom* is a generative book. It ignites the prophetic imagination and calls us to participate in God's mission of healing and liberating broken creation."

— CHERYL BRIDGES JOHNS
Pentecostal Theological Seminary

DEFIANT

*What the Women of Exodus
Teach Us about Freedom*

Kelley Nikondeha

WILLIAM B. EERDMANS PUBLISHING COMPANY
GRAND RAPIDS, MICHIGAN

Wm. B. Eerdmans Publishing Co.
4035 Park East Court SE, Grand Rapids, Michigan 49546
www.eerdmans.com

ISBN 978-0-8028-6429-1

Library of Congress Cataloging-in-Publication Data

Names: Nikondeha, Kelley, 1969– author.
Title: Defiant : what the women of Exodus teach us about freedom / Kelley
    Nikondeha.
Description: Grand Rapids, Michigan : William B. Eerdmans Publishing
    Company, 2020. | Summary: "Looking back to the women of Exodus as
    well as to women around the world today, this book presents a para-
    digm for women that highlights the biblical mandate to join the libera-
    tion work in our world"— Provided by publisher.
Identifiers: LCCN 2019044037 | ISBN 9780802864291 (paperback)
Subjects: LCSH: Bible. Exodus—Criticism, interpretation, etc. | Women in
    the Bible. | Liberty—Religious aspects—Christianity.
Classification: LCC BS1245.52 .N55 2020 | DDC 222/.12092082—dc23
LC record available at https://lccn.loc.gov/2019044037

2023-11

*For all the women who want to know
what faithfulness looks like in perilous times.*

*And for D. L. Mayfield, Elie Pritz,
Kaitlin Curtice, and Lisa Sharon Harper—defiant women
who show me what faithfulness looks like here and now.*

Contents

CONTENTS

Foreword

I have never forgotten the first time I heard Kelley talk about
the women of Exodus. She hadn't imagined it being a book
just yet; she was still knee-deep in her own learning (because
this is how Kelley has fun: commentaries, deep-dive research,
and repeated listening to Walter Brueggemann sermons). We
were at a friend's house, four of us eating peaches and making
plans together. We were workshopping our callings, figuring
out how to do the work we felt God had called us to do, helping
one another discern and dream. If there is one thing that dangerous women like to do, it is making dangerous plans together.

When it was her turn to share about the work she wanted
to lean into next, Kelley stood up from the red couch where
she had been reclining next to Tina and steadied herself by lay-
ing one hand on the piano as she began to share. Our dialogue
ceased as the words you are about to read poured forth from her
soul. We stopped moving, stopped talking, stopped breathing
(or so it seemed). Kelley was lit up with a light of revelation. I
had the weirdest instinct to take off my shoes as if she were cre-

ating holy ground with her words. By the time she was finished sharing about the women of Exodus, I nearly got up and ran a lap around the neighborhood. I remember looking at the other two in the room and saying, "Did we just hear the best sermon of our entire lives right here in this living room? Freestyled beside the piano?"

Kelley introduced me to a narrative of liberative, connected women that utterly captured my imagination, and I've never gotten over it. I have been deeply transformed by Kelley's witness to these women. Walking alongside of her as she first delved into the concept, through her meticulous deep research, to the thoughtful prophetic result has been like having a front seat to a masterclass in theological writing that can actually transform lives. Her theological imagination, honesty, depth, wisdom, and embodied power is a song of freedom for all of us. She is such a good guide for you on the path of liberation. She served as a midwife to this message, she mothered it, and now she's ready to pass it along to us as the next link in what she calls The Nile Network of solidarity. Get ready.

For too long the notion of biblical womanhood has felt weak and ineffectual, a cookie-cutter vision of a 1950s sitcom that didn't even exist in real life, and yet it crippled and silenced generations of women in the church. In *Defiant*, Kelley lays out a feast for us of the truth about biblical womanhood: the resistance, the strength, the civil disobedience, the collaboration, the truth-telling, the drumming, the wit, the holy liberated power of women who know their God. She connects everything she learned from the women of Exodus to the women of our past and our time whose subversive strength continues to spell the downfall of evil and injustice. In these pages, you will learn to recognize women at work. This book is more than permission;

it's a clear call to rise up to the Exodus mandate for all of us. In these pages we begin to see that the blueprints of our liberation have been here all along.

I believe that this book has important work to do in the world—it could not be more timely, more relevant, more necessary for women to read and understand this story and our place within it. I'm grateful to Kelley for her faithfulness to this work because I believe that if we listen, if we open our hands and our hearts to discern what the Holy Spirit is saying to us in these pages, it will mean transformation not only in our own lives but in our communities, our marriages, our churches, our neighborhoods, and the generations coming up behind us.

SARAH BESSEY
author of *Jesus Feminist*
and *Miracles and Other*
Reasonable Things

Introduction

I grew up in Orange County, California, when its namesake was obvious. Rows and rows of orange trees surrounded the El Toro marine base, and each spring the groves perfumed the air with orange-blossom goodness that overpowered the exhaust from the nearby 405 freeway. The Blue Angels flew high above the base for annual air shows. My parents would pull our car to the side of the road, the grove side, and we would pop our heads back full tilt and watch the silver jets cut the sky in two.

Around this time my parents left the Catholic Church, taking me with them. I remember my mom grumbling about their veneration of Mary, among other things that upset her. We entered the evangelical church when I was still in elementary school. Gone was Mother Mary. Instead I discovered a lesser role for women, more constricted and gendered. Girls grew up to be wives and mothers. Good Christian women married men who would be leaders of the family, while the women managed the household. My own parents functioned in quite egalitarian ways, which always felt wonderfully subversive. But my mother's freedom at home did not exempt her from the more limited roles for women in congregational life.

The church expected women to be like Martha, who made the meals, set the table, and hosted Jesus and his disciples. No matter what they said in the occasional sermon about her sister Mary, who "chose the better thing" by sitting at the feet of Jesus, their structures and practices made it clear that women belonged elsewhere. Women were meant to be submissive and genteel and mostly sequestered in the domestic realm. Our place was in the kitchen, not in the pulpit or the leadership structure of the congregation.

I could have used Mother Mary in my youth to remind me that along with mothering, a woman could sing of grand reversals and dream of freedom from poverty and oppression. Like her, women could contemplate deeply, accompany others through hardship, bear witness to loss, and compose liberation songs. Perhaps she would have whispered to me that a woman's place was also in the resistance. In retrospect, I think I always missed Mother Mary and her Magnificat.

◆　　　◆　　　◆

My mother, industrious despite her chronic and undiagnosed illness, oversaw the women's ministry of our church. She recruited women to Reach-Touch-Serve and deployed them. They would bring meals to those who had just come home from the hospital, clean houses for those too sick to get out of bed, and help with childcare when mothers were the ones in bed. They hosted all the fundraisers for missions, summer camp, and whatever else the pastor requested—fashion shows, chili cook-offs, bake sales, and the holiday bazaar, where they sold homemade crafts. The women of Reach-Touch-Serve also decorated the sanctuary for Christmas and hosted all special events in the fellowship hall next door. So many days my mom was the first to arrive at church, armed with clipboards and lists, and then the last to leave, carting boxes filled with soiled table linens, Pyrex dishes, and the metal cashbox. Her work never ended and our phone was always ringing. But seldom did my mom complain. I marveled at her work ethic and her heart for the church.

My mom met Margret at a seminar hosted by another local church. Margret cried out, to use the language of Exodus, desperate for some kind of relief from her pain. My mother heard and started bringing her around. From my adolescent perspective, Margret towered over my mother. And she always looked tired, like smiling took all her available energy. Margret was unlike any of the other women who surrounded my mom. She was married to an addict who abused her. She was trying to get out, get away, maybe even divorce. She was mired in the kind of messes my mom typically avoided.

My mother embraced Margret. She went to her dingy apartment on the hard edge of town and sat with her. She took her to lunch and shared in conversation. She saw Margret and her pain. And she did all she could to walk with Margret, for many months, through the hard work of leaving her husband—even though my mother hates divorce. She was there to empty Margret's apartment, drive her to the airport, and send her home where she could be free. I was never more proud of my mother than when I saw her love Margret. The Spirit worked to set Margret free from an abusive relationship, and my mother was a midwife.

I saw Margret set free. All these years later what I remember is Margret, not the women's ministry my mother led for seven years. Her freedom was compelling, even though I didn't have the insight back then to call it *freedom*. All I knew was that women's ministry wasn't a magnet like this other thing—liberation—was.

• • •

The military base closed in 1999—the same year I graduated from seminary. By then all the orange groves had vanished, making way for suburban subdivisions, shopping malls, and parking lots. I drove the old roads to and from seminary classes, mindlessly passing the chained-up base entrances as I parsed Hebrew verbs, rehearsed the differences between the creation narratives in Genesis, and considered Pauline arguments regarding women in the church. Sometimes, usually at night while heading home, I rolled down my car window in the hope of catching even a faint whiff of the orange blossoms. But they were long gone by then.

I was entering my thirties, soon to marry and become a mother. My axis was about to radically shift. I married Claude, born and raised in Burundi, and found myself in a bicultural (and eventually bicontinental) marriage with someone who experienced another side of the world. He had survived colonization, poverty, tribal hatred, and civil war. Both his suffering and his survival began to dismantle my easy answers, pushing me toward the challenges of a complex world groaning for restoration. We adopted two Burundian babies, one orphaned by HIV/AIDS and the other orphaned by extreme poverty. Adoption is a sacrament of both love and lament, so while we learned how to practice belonging as a newly formed family, we also learned to hold space for the sadness of losing birth parents and cultural connection. Justin and Emma made us parents; they also made us advocates for families at risk. Several years later we would start a community development enterprise in Burundi, Communities of Hope, to "convert unjust communities into just ones," as Gustavo Gutiérrez once said.

As a woman navigating both church and community, my task at hand was to learn where I fit in the work of God on earth. I knew that women's ministry, serving in the nursery, or teaching children in Sunday school was not for me. Even though I married an ordained pastor, I couldn't see myself following in the footsteps of the pastor's wives I'd known across the years. Most wore floral dresses in pastel colors and were soft-spoken. As Claude observed, they would sit on the stage or in the front row and "just look pretty." That was not me. I loved to preach. I was a thinker and a leader. I didn't fit the prescribed roles for women in the church. There were no models who sparked my imagination.

So I kept the models who nourished me from my youth— Moses chief among them. Maybe because we were both adopted and wrestled with our identity shaped at the intersection of nature and nurture, I felt a kinship with him. I also loved that he was an emancipator of the enslaved. His vocation was liberation. That compelled me. Jesus captivated me. I loved how Jesus set people free from sickness, social stigma, debt, and other kinds of poverty. Jesus wove the liberation thread through Palestinian streets and into the very fabric of the New Testament. And there was always Mother Mary gently haunting me.

As I meditated on the Exodus narrative over the years, I began to notice other liberation practitioners at work. Midwives stood up to Pharaoh by defying his death order targeting baby boys. Jochebed took the risk of giving birth in Egypt and hiding her son until she could come up with a plan to save him. Pharaoh's daughter collaborated with the Hebrew women by adopting the boy, another act of salvation. Young Miriam was both clever and courageous as she negotiated a wet-nurse contract between these women, her own contribution to the rescue operation. In her adulthood, she would function as a community organizer capable of leading the women and partnering with her brothers. Zipporah and her sisters exemplified solidarity in the hard desert landscape, and she even saved Moses's life as they made their way back to Egypt. These women created the conditions for liberation over decades. They saved Moses, and they taught him what liberation practices look like.

It occurred to me that these women provide us with a good archetype for the work of women in the church and world today. Our generation of women needs to see the mothers of the liberation movement who've gone before us with such strength and stamina. Watching them, we can imagine fresh possibilities for how to engage in faithful ways amid chaotic times. The Exodus women crack open our imagination, and the Spirit leads us as she led our foremothers. We get to participate in the liberation work of our day—in our youth or advanced age, as mothers, as unmarried women, as wives and sisters, whether we are the ones hemmed in by injustice or the ones with privilege. The Exodus story is our story.

The Exodus women function as an archetype for the work of modern women in two ways. First, all the various actions of the women are available to us today. We can defy the pharaohs (and pharaonic policies) of our day; we can subvert ordinary tasks for salvific purpose; we can organize for resistance and work in solidarity to repair our neighborhoods. We can be the kind of women who talk with our neighbors and practice reparations so that we can all be free and live viable and vibrant lives. And what the Exodus women did is not a comprehensive list of liberation activity; this is just a place to begin envisioning the variety of ways the Spirit invites us into the work of emancipation.

Second, the Exodus women challenge us to consider our social location. In this narrative we see Hebrew women oppressed by the edicts of the empire. We encounter women of privilege, like Pharaoh's daughter. Some women are at risk while others live in relative ease. The Egyptian system enslaved some families and benefited others. Where are we in relation to our own systems? Are we oppressed? Do we recognize the privilege we have due to our lighter skin color or higher education or our position on the socioeconomic ladder? Often it isn't either-or but more complex as we see the various roles we play in our homes, churches, and communities at large. What does our social position require of us in regard to liberative practice? The Exodus narrative asks a series of important questions about our social location in and around empires as we watch these women at work.

●   ●   ●

I explore the women in the Exodus narrative as a student of Scripture and a woman hungry for justice. My method for this book is rather simple: exegesis, meditation, and imagination. I study Exodus and related Scriptures as any diligent exegete would—reading commentaries and the work of scholars steeped in these ancient texts. I also meditate on these passages, returning to them time and time again to see what the Spirit will reveal. Over the last several years, I've traveled with a wide-lined text of Exodus in my carry-on as I visited Israel-Palestine,

Kenya, Uganda, Rwanda, Burundi, and the United States. The stories of these women have worked me over season by season, place by place, gently giving up their wisdom.

And then there is the place of my imagination in the theological work at hand. Dr. Wilda Gafney says her tradition calls this using your "sanctified imagination." When you become close to the Scripture narrative through study and meditation, your imagination becomes engaged and privy to the work of the Spirit. So I share my own imagining in this book—how I envision these women in connection with one another, and even some of the conversations they might have shared together. Sometimes it helps to consider what it looked like then so that we can imagine what it might look like for us to embody the same kind of liberation work in our current context. My imagination is inspired by the text, by my proximity to these women, and, I hope, by the Spirit. So again, this exploration of Exodus braids together exegesis, meditation, and imagination, and I pray it is profitable for our conversation.

Now we turn to the women of Exodus. What can they teach us about practicing liberation in Egypt so that we may practice liberation in our world? How might these women empower us as we seek to work in the church and throughout our communities? These women have been hidden for too long. I believe they have wisdom to impart for times such as these, because like Margret, we all want to be free. I believe these women, who most likely inspired Mary's Magnificat, can inspire us to sing new freedom songs. They show us that women's work can look like defying Pharaoh, raising Moses, and plundering Egypt.

Chapter 1

TWELVE MEN, TWELVE WOMEN

The Nile River teemed with life. Fish shimmied through the waters—sleek tiger fish and silver perch, schools of tilapia, ribbon-like eels, and all manner of catfish, roaming the watery depths. Along the shores a lounging crocodile could be seen, and soft-shelled turtles, frogs, lizards, and even bulbous hippos gliding downstream. And birds—everywhere birds. You could see them in the air, flying toward the sun or scavenging closer to the water's surface. The delta was a fertile place—even for the Hebrews.

Indeed, the first glimpse we get of this people group in the book of Exodus shows them as fruitful, multiplying and filling the land. The idyllic opening scene is a picture of the kind of life the Creator promised humanity back in the garden.

Joseph, brought by force as a slave many generations ago, had risen to prominence in Egypt. His strategic contributions to the imperial house had staved off a potentially dire food shortage amid famine in the region. Joseph's successful management of the food crisis had opened the door for his father and brothers to migrate to Egypt with the pharaoh's blessing.[1] This is how Israel's family tree, chock-full of dreams, brothers, and forgiveness, took root in the Fertile Crescent. Or so the story goes.

After Joseph and his brothers died, the family lived on. As a matter of fact, they grew strong in their adopted homeland. The narrator of Exodus tells us that "the Israelites were *fruitful* and *prolific*; they *multiplied* and *grew exceedingly strong*, so that the land was *filled* with them."[2] Packed in this single verse are seven words describing the dramatic and enduring increase of this family.[3] No one listening to the story could mistake the clear signal of this sevenfold strength. The creation-level goodness manifests before our very eyes.

From Genesis to the opening scene of Exodus, creation continues with fertile force. With those creation notes sounding in Exodus 1:7—notes of fruitfulness, of teeming life, of land that is filled—we're meant to be momentarily transported back to that lush garden where original shalom was established and all was right.

This is where the story of Exodus begins—not in a brickyard but in a garden. It's not the backbreaking work, relentless quotas, and crack of the whip that set the scene. That will unfold soon enough. Instead, our first sighting of the Hebrews is edenic, with connotations of delight and goodness. Before we see their slavery, we see their humanity. Flourishing comes first.

While we're reflecting on beginnings, it's worth remembering that men and women, created in God's image, possess the capacity for dominion. This means that each person can "exercise agency to steward God's creation."[4] Lisa Sharon Harper notes that Genesis 1 "makes no distinction between the kind of dominion that males and females are called to exercise. There is only the call to exercise co-dominion, to steward the earth, to protect and serve the rest of creation together."[5] So from the beginning, women have agency to shape society, as do their male counterparts. Shalom is a joint endeavor.

Men are not intended to have one-sided dominion over women. Likewise, Egyptians are not meant to rule over Hebrews and deny them their God-given work of dominion. All peoples are equally created and tasked to shape their communities toward shalom. When one group oppresses another, the Exodus story demonstrates that men and women have a mandate to participate in liberation to restore shalom for all.

●　　　●　　　●

If you are familiar with the book of Exodus, you know that I skipped the long string of names at the beginning. I began with the most verdant image, but let's return to the first words of the story and listen to the logic of the narrator. The book begins, "These are the names of the sons of Israel who came to Egypt with Jacob . . ."[6] The narrator lists the names of the twelve sons of Jacob.[7] These were the ones who traveled from Canaan to escape famine, the ones who settled in Goshen, the rich land to the east of the Nile River. And it is their progeny who are now living that shalom life under the Egyptian sun.

The names are important to the Israelites, but so is the number twelve. This is a number that carries the weight of tribal leadership, not just for Israelites but also for many of the regional powers. There were the twelve chieftains of Ishmael, the twelve sons of Nahor, and an Edomite league of rulers organized by twelve[8]—all leadership collectives in the denomination of twelve. So when the narrator starts with the twelve names of

Jacob's sons, we are seeing not only genealogy at work but also the leadership structure of Hebrew society. In accordance with ancient cultural norms, the list is made of all male names.

So our story proper starts with the names of twelve men. It is obvious that these men had mothers. Israelites would have known their names: Leah, Rachel, Bilhah, and Zilpah. These women gave birth to those twelve; they nursed them and raised them into men. Leah and Rachel died in Canaan. But it seems likely that Bilhah and Zilpah (along with the lone daughter, Dinah) sojourned into Egypt with Jacob. They are a part of the story, even if shrouded by patriarchy. So when I see the twelve names of their sons, I remember to say their names too.

As we circle back to Jacob's family, consider that no increase would have been possible without the women. They conceived, gestated life in their bellies, gave birth, and raised these children. Mothers are a formative force in any society, whether they are part of the twelve names or not. So while their names are sidelined in history, I think of them as a vital part of the increase of the Hebrews. They are the women who've left an imprint on the story before we've even begun. The narrator has barely spoken a word, merely some names, and already we benefit from the contribution of women, who keep their families nourished and the fires burning in the cool evening hours by the Nile's edge.

•　　•　　•

A well-known fact in community development circles is that if you want to enter a community, you introduce yourself to the leader, most often a man. But if you want to learn how the community functions and tap into its life force, then make time to listen to the women. The key to transformation is found among the women. When my husband, Claude, and I began our work in Burundi, I didn't yet fully grasp this fundamental truth.

In 2009, our fledgling development organization began work in the gentle green mountains of Matara, a rural commune about eleven miles from the capital city. Working with community leaders, we identified and invited thirty Batwa families to move to a new plot of land that would become theirs. On a hot June day, the men arrived from other provinces with little more than a single sack of essentials—all they owned, really. They surveyed the land and all the work that would need to be done to make it home and to bring about food security for their families sooner rather than later. It was daunting. One man gave up after a couple of days; another was out in a week's time. But to their credit, the balance of the men got to work clearing land.

In the first week of July, their wives and children joined them. Again, they came with little in the way of possessions. For most of the mothers (they were all mothers), the bright-colored *igitenge* wrapped around their waist was the most valuable item they owned.[9] As they entered the camp, I assumed they would cook and care for the children and maybe try to turn the tents into makeshift homes for their families. I thought they came too soon and would slow down the progress, burdening the men with additional worries as they worked. I knew next to nothing about development work, as my early assumptions revealed.

When I visited a couple of weeks later with Claude, I saw a winding ribbon of color in the distant field. As we walked down toward the action, I could hear the chatter. I began to see the women, wrapped in their *ibitenge*, swinging hoes over their shoulders into the dark soil. I counted twenty-two women laboring in the sun. Once we made it to the field, I noticed that many of the women had a baby strapped to their back. The next time I visited the women of Matara, I found them, again, in ribbon-like formation, planting cabbage. They pointed out where they'd just finished planting row upon row of carrots. They wore babies—and smiles.

I'm sure they were motivated to drop seeds and hasten the harvest—this would be the first time the bounty belonged to them. But their work ethic took me by surprise nonetheless. I'd never witnessed this kind of feminine labor force. My Batwa friends were educating me in the capacity and commitment of women. The fieldwork was only the beginning. In the coming seasons they would take leadership roles at the local school advocating for education; they would organize the harvest and food storage; they would try their hand at livestock (rabbits first, then chickens and pigs). They accomplished all this while caring for their husbands and children—and one another.

The women shaped their new society on the hills of Matara. It came naturally to them, or so it seemed to me as an observer. I mean no disrespect to the men; they were no slackers. But the daily contribution of the women was undeniable. Their efforts focused on family health and the well-being of their neighbors. With energy they attempted things and proved they were more equipped than I had known.

The original leadership committee established in Matara consisted of twelve men. We wanted the Batwa families involved in the direction and management of their community from the very beginning, so in keeping with local tradition, twelve men were selected. Eighteen months later, it was time for an election of new leaders. In the intervening months, the families had planted and seen their first harvest, the school-age children had attended the school across the road, and everyone was getting stronger with each meal and regular access to medical care. The families voted. They elected three men—and Leonie and Jacqueline.[10] Despite a culture with a strong preference for male leadership, the women were obvious partners in the creation of this new home. Everyone saw it and affirmed it—including Claude and me.

This was the first time I walked in Eden. The land awash in hues of green I'd never seen before. Color-block fabrics moving in the golden sun, trees heavy with yellow banana clusters and blushing mangoes against a sapphire sky. Each step transported me. When we arrived, the women were singing, whistle trills punctuating their songs and babies still onboard. They danced, their bare feet pounding the ground like a drum. We were celebrating another anniversary together, another year in which, as François announced, "no one died." Another year in which everyone ate, drank clean water from the local stream, and more babies were born. So many babies! I mention this because I don't want you to miss it. This is what original shalom looks like—a collection of families fruitful and multiplying and filling their land. It's men and women working together in creation goodness—and it is possible in Egypt or Matara or wherever you find yourself.

The Batwa tribe is a marginalized minority in Burundi, often subjected to harassment and humiliation at the hands of Tutsis and Hutus. Extreme poverty and discrimination were all these women knew. In her anniversary speech, Leonie positioned herself into a tiny ball, covered in a dirty, torn *igitenge*. Then she sprang up, dropping the tattered fabric to reveal her bright *igitenge* and radiant countenance. "Now I know I am human," she announced. In the fields of Matara, she and her sisters discovered their humanity and their capacity. They awoke to their own agency and power to effect change—then they got to work. Without cracking open a single community development primer, these women schooled me.

•   •   •

Watching the women of Matara helped me to recognize my own assumptions, shaped by American evangelical culture, that women are the side dish and not the main. We are gathered at the periphery, leaving plenty of space for men to take the spotlight. This was especially true in church, where men stood in the pulpit and made up the elder board and women were not allowed to serve even as deacons. The men cast the vision and led the charge while the women set the tables, brought the casseroles, and looked after the children. The message I got growing up was that women flourished in support roles.

American history books contain stories of women who changed society with their hard work and insistence on justice. The women of the suffrage movement clad in white, those active in the temperance movement, and those advocating for better housing and protections for children contributed to the formation of our nation. I can name the abolitionist Harriet Tubman of the Underground Railroad; Jane Addams, who started the settlement house movement in America along with other social work initiatives; Dorothy Day of the Catholic Worker Movement; and Dolores Huerta of the United Farm Workers in California. But I confess that these women, some of whom I studied during my school years, seemed to be extraordinary exceptions when it came to my own perception of women. No one told me that this kind of strength and determination was common to all women.

Witnessing the Batwa women challenged what I thought I knew about men and women and work. Their strength was a catalyst for my own concept of what is possible for women. Thanks to them, I saw the muscle in other women across the city of Bujumbura. They managed fruit stands by day and cooked and cared for children by night. They ran banks or factories or NGOs during the week and served in church on Sundays. I saw what the development manuals spoke of: the deep reliability of women and their capacity to transform communities. The women took their own lived experience, the joy and the suffering, and extracted insight about what needed to happen in their homes and neighborhoods. They used what was on hand, what spaces were available to them, and set about solving problems. From the stuff of their very life, they began to spin thread and stitch something good.

The mothers of Matara embodied a dynamic beyond the pages of any book, allowing me to contemplate for the first time the full dimension of women. They calibrated my vision to see the full potential of women in the church and in the community at large. I began to survey my own territory with a fresh lens, noticing women as never before. Women hold up half the sky—and I finally recognized it. Maybe that is why I could at last see the women of Exodus.

The Hebrew women operated in the shadows of the men, but now I was learning to see them. I no longer stopped at the list of twelve names. In Burundi, I looked beyond the long shadow cast by patriarchy and found women hard at work in their families and neighborhoods. They were holding together life. I even noticed it in my North American context for the first time. Women cooked, cleaned, and drove carpool—I knew as much. But then I saw how they supported the local school with donated supplies and volunteer hours, attended city-planning meetings to save the neighborhood park, gave to the food bank, and checked in on their aging parents. Everywhere I looked I saw women as active contributors to the health of their communities. In many instances they made life not only viable but also vibrant.

Realizing what women do in the world and at home made me think of the good churchwomen I knew. Plenty of women filled the pews each week at Sunday services. They also did much of the serving: running children's programs, overseeing the altar guild, planning the many events in the fellowship hall—and often providing the food. But too many were limited to tasks that fell under the canopy of "women's ministry," the softer side of ministry. I began to think our wings had been clipped. If women were able to help bring about food security for an entire community, then certainly we could organize and tackle more significant challenges that plague our neighborhoods once again. We could be energized for work beyond the home front, work that would bring goodness to many other homes in our neighborhood. What if women in ministry looked more like the women in Matara, our energy harnessed to end child hunger in our city or support under-resourced schools or actively assist in local refugee resettlement to make our new neighbors feel at home? What if there were a wider-scale movement of churchwomen engaged in work that benefits not only their local church family but also the wider neighborhood? What I know now is that we possess the requisite capacity to bring more than the hot dish. We are half the church, and we can partner in liberation work both inside and outside our communities.[11]

•　　　•　　　•

Luke saw the capacity of women more than most, at least more than his fellow Gospel writers, Matthew, Mark, and John. Luke saw women not only receive from the ministry of Jesus but also give to it. All the Gospel men testify to the presence of Mary Magdalene, Mary the mother of James, and Salome, all of whom followed Jesus from Galilee to Jerusalem. They were at the foot of the cross and at the tomb of Jesus in the garden. You can't talk about the resurrection without the women. But Luke also mentions certain women who were with Jesus as he traveled to the many villages around Galilee during his teaching years. Mary Magdalene, Joanna, Susanna, and other women kept company with the rabbi. They provided for Jesus and the twelve disciples out of their resources.[12]

We've been taught that these were wealthy women. Certain women in any society will have the riches combined with the luxury of time to support charities or ministries—these were the ones who supported Jesus & Company. Somehow, speaking about them as wealthy women sets them apart from most of us average women who have to work, at home or outside it, but never achieve enough wealth to be a major donor to the work of Jesus. Just as certain women got to support Jesus and tag along, certain women today get to be part of the ministry of the church—a select few get to stand in the pulpit or lead a mission initiative or, in a rare instance, be installed as a deacon. But only *certain women*. This is how I was taught to understand the preaching of Anne Graham Lotz and Beth Moore and, further back, women like Aimee Semple McPherson, Mother Teresa, Dorothy Sayers, and Madeleine L'Engle. They were anomalies, the exception, not the rule, when it came to the role women got to play in the ministry of Jesus—then and now. If you weren't rich with money or unquestionable talent or an undoubted anointing, then you were relegated to a support role in church work.

But what if our assumptions are wrong about these women? Renita Weems notes that "undoubtedly women from all economic backgrounds—the wealthy, the comfortable, the modest, the poor, and the homeless—were changed by Jesus' ministry."[13] Would they stop with receiving—or might they want to give something in return to the rabbi who healed them, cast out their demons, or honored their desire to be part of the conversations about God's kingdom?

And what if, as Weems suggests, the women then were like the women today? What if they were women rich in commitment, not money? "Dedicated women are certainly the women who have been the financial spinal column of the black church—not rich women, but generous women, women who give all they have, even when what they have is just a little."[14] What if the point isn't that certain women are wealthy but that many women are dedicated to Jesus and willing to support the work of his church with their time, talent, energy, and, yes, money, to see the good news spread from town to town? When I recall the churches I've been a part of over the years, the women outnumbered the men. They also outpaced their male counterparts in volunteer hours, always showing up early and staying late to support the work. The good churchmen could not have kept the congregation afloat without the dedication of the women. This isn't a contest but a call to recognize the dedication of women as a treasure of the church. When all women are invited into the full work of the church—with their heart, mind, soul, and strength—imagine what strongholds could be torn down.

◆　　◆　　◆

Back in Matara there were squabbles between families, marital strife, and sometimes mismanagement of resources. This community was no utopia—no community is. They are beset by all the maladies that befall humans—greed, selfishness, and fear among them. But there are moments of shalom worth seeing. If we hold on to these shalom sightings, it might allow us to tap into a sustainable creation-like energy with which to tackle the hardships that come our way. We can hope the same for those along the Nile Delta, because the story is about to take an unexpected turn.

"A new king arose over Egypt, who did not know Joseph."[15] It sounds ominous—because it is. No one expected this twist after lingering in the goodness of Goshen. But a new pharaoh has come to power, one who does not recognize Joseph or his contributions to the state or that the previous pharaoh blessed the Hebrew migration. It's hard to imagine that he did not know, and more likely that he exercised a selective amnesia. In forgetting Joseph, he could forget the policies of his predecessor, abandon state commitments, and revoke privileges previously granted to Jacob and sons.[16] Shalom shattered in an instant.

In the first spoken words of Exodus, we hear of Pharaoh's preoccupation: "Look, the Israelite people are more numerous and more powerful than we."[17] No surprise that Pharaoh is fixated on numbers and greatness—this is the Achilles' heel of pharaohs to this day. They are threatened by other people and ignorant of their own histories. Seeing the "many and mighty" Hebrews,[18] Pharaoh decided to curb their fecundity with hard labor.

The Hebrews were conscripted into Pharaoh's building enterprise. "But," says the narrator, "the more they were oppressed, the more they multiplied and spread."[19] The plan wasn't working. Instead of diminishing them, the oppression somehow caused an increase. And this was when the Egyptians, in agreement with their pharaoh, began to dread the Hebrews. The taskmasters became ruthless in the brickyards. Egyptians hammered the Hebrews with long hours of hard service.[20]

So far, the narrator has not mentioned the women. But I imagine them suffering in the shadows. Injustice always hits the women hardest. From abundance to scarcity, the women worked to keep the family together with fewer resources and less energetic participation from their male counterparts, who spent it all making bricks for the master. They weren't in the garden anymore—and the women knew it.

•   •   •

Until recently, most Americans didn't know that women were pivotal to the NASA space program as far back as the 1950s. Their names and accomplishments were lost to the common history we grew up studying. Aerospace exploits seemed the exclusive territory of men—the scientists, engineers, and astronauts. But the movie *Hidden Figures*[21] brought these women's names front and center. We learned that Katherine Johnson made the critical calculations necessary for John Glenn to successfully land in Project Mercury. Her work as a mathematician would contribute to many more missions, including Apollo 11 and the space shuttle program. Dorothy Vaughan was also a mathematician, as well as the first black supervisor at NASA—one of the few women in that role. She taught herself FORTRAN, a computing language, before she went on to teach her entire team how to program and was installed as the head of the programming division at NASA. Mary Jackson was a mathematician and an aerospace engineer with a long career at NASA. In addition to her computing skills, she served as the manager of both the Federal Women's Program and the Affirmative Action Program at NASA to advocate for women in hiring and advancement within the organization. She didn't just make her own way in a man's world; she made a way for other women to join her.

These three brilliant African American women helped shape America's aerospace program, yet we almost missed them in the landscape of male names. They weren't invisible to their coworkers or their families. Colleagues knew they were doing nearly impossible calculations, saving the day on more than one grand occasion, all the while advancing aerospace with their human computing skills. Someone at home knew they worked through lunch and late into the night. People knew they were making the crooked roads a little straighter for other women. However, their stories weren't told in the official annals of the Space Race. We didn't see their faces in the sepia highlight reels of all those amazing launches and landings. This is how patriarchy works: a fixed focus on the accomplishments of men and the minimization or erasure of women's contributions.

Imagine if we didn't know their names. We'd still be under the illusion that aerospace is the territory of men. We'd think that the foundational contributions to NASA were all made by men and that men won the Space Race. But that was never the whole truth of how we accomplished that victory in space. Women were always part of the story—we just didn't see them, by design.

I believe the same can be said for the Exodus narrative. We think this epic story is the terrain of men—in particular, Moses. The names that lead off the book set the expected trajectory for liberation. The twelve sons, Israel's twelve chiefs, will be the actors in this movement, we might assume. But the narrator knows better. Maybe watching his own mother at work in her community opened his eyes to see her contribution. Maybe that led him to recognize the other women woven into the epic movement out of Egypt. Soon enough he will introduce us to two women by name, and then ten more women throughout the deliverance narrative.[22] Twelve women engaged in the emancipation work—another leadership structure operating in the shadows of the brickyards.

These twelve women are the hidden figures of the liberation movement. What we will see are women laboring on the frontlines, creating the conditions for liberation. Without the subversive strength, clever strategies, and solidarity of the women, Moses would not have survived Egypt. These women—midwives and mothers, Miriam in her youth and advanced age, even Hebrew women collaborating with Egyptian neighbors—made exodus possible.

There have always been twelve men atop the leadership structures of the world, in families, and in the church. We see this in Exodus with Jacob and sons, in the inaugural leadership committee in Matara, and even in the disciples Jesus chose. But the twelve men are never the full story. There will always be certain women working behind the scenes, committed and talented and called to exercise their agency too. They have not always been known or named, but they've held families and communities together. Even more, these women labored for liberation for their families and neighbors. True liberation isn't possible without the full participation of women. Now more than ever we need to remember and accept the Exodus invitation.

Sadly, the dozen men dwarf the few women time and time again. We are outnumbered—not because there are fewer women available, though. Too often we don't see the women already at work among us, expending their energies toward justice for their families and local communities. When this happens, we miss out on their good example and the chance to be both inspired by and recruited into liberation work. The second factor is that many of us haven't taken our place in the liberation movement yet. We sit on the sidelines. Maybe we don't know that the liberation landscape is ours too. What I hope is that we will see the women practicing liberation and join them.

What we will witness in the liberation story of Exodus is that there were twelve men—and twelve women—working toward liberation. What we will see here is that it takes the full complement of humanity to break free from Pharaoh. The twelve women of Exodus become our archetype of women at work, exerting their shared dominion not only in creation but also in liberation.

Chapter 2

SHIPHRAH AND PUAH

Freedom through Disobedience

The atmosphere among the midwives must have been tense when the mighty king summoned two of their own to come at once to the royal court. "Has this ever happened before?" the midwives in training must have asked their elders. Shiphrah and Puah were, in all likelihood, not the only two midwives for the entire group of fertile Hebrews. They were the leaders of the midwifery guild in Goshen.[1] "What possible interest could he have in our business of delivering babies?" the other midwives asked, crowded together as they awaited the return of the women.

The king spoke at last. He addressed Shiphrah and Puah with instructions for their ongoing work among their kinswomen. "When you deliver their babies, if you see that it is a boy, kill it." Then he added, "If it's a girl, let her live."[2] They were dismissed without any further explanation. No one argues with the pharaoh; you simply obey. And thereby Pharaoh launched into his next plan to curb the proliferation of the insects plaguing him.

Earlier the writer of Exodus describes the Hebrews as possessing a sevenfold strength.[3] One of the words used to describe their fruitfulness, *teeming*, echoes the creation narrative in Genesis in which the newly created waters are teeming, or swarming, with life. This sense of the Hebrew word is positive. But in other contexts it can carry a negative connotation, and that's certainly how Pharaoh interprets the Hebrews' teeming—as akin to the swarming of insects. Such disdainful language is similar to that used in the Rwandan genocide, the Hutus calling the Tutsis cockroaches.[4] It's familiar to us in the mouth of more recent leaders in America who have called people animals and have described immigrants as "infesting" our nation. It's the vernacular of dehumanization, and it will come into play in the Exodus story soon enough, though we feel it in the undercurrent here, when the king commands killing as if these people were insects and not baby boys.

◆   ◆   ◆

In Hebraic fashion, the narrator tells us who is, and isn't, consequential in this scene. Unlike Jacob and his twelve sons, all of whom are called out by name in the exposition, the king has no name. And once the action kicks off, it is Shiphrah and Puah who receive the honor of a named mention. We are meant to pay close attention to the midwives.[5] Rulers come and go; their names hardly matter. But commit the names of these women, Shiphrah and Puah, to memory. They are about to effect a grand reversal of their own.

We don't know much about the two women, except that they are remembered as Hebrew midwives. Hebrew wasn't an ethnic designation so much as a socioeconomic one. Hebrews were the lowlifes of society, often living on the margins and without resources or respect. One commentator notes that Egyptian texts of the period refer to slaves in general as Hebrews.[6] So it was that the children of Israel took a turn from shalom to slavery and are known as Hebrews for the remainder of the Exodus story, with few exceptions. This is a story preoccupied with those on the bottom rung of the socioeconomic ladder.

Shiphrah and Puah worked in the margins of the empire. But as midwives, they were held in high regard in their community. They were skilled women with wisdom about maternal and infant health, hands able to deliver babies, and hearts of compassion able to soothe anxious mothers.[7] Tender and tough in turn, their gift of discernment must have been well honed. As co-chairs of the midwifery guild, they would have also been teachers, mentors, and leaders. The king, no doubt, put emphasis on their lowly Hebrew status, but their neighbors would have recognized their standing as midwives. So these women worked between these assumptions, most days unconcerned with the king's opinion of them as they went about their business. Until the day he summoned them, expecting their obedience.

The midwives left the palace complex in a hurry. In the very next breath the narrator tells us that Shiphrah and Puah feared God, not the king. This is a statement not about their belief but about their practice, as we are about to see.[8] As they rushed back to their neighborhood, neither one entertained the notion of participating in the king's covert operation. The God of life would be obeyed, even if it meant disobeying the ruler of the land.

I can only imagine what it must have been like in the room on the south side of the delta as the sun dropped low and the women awaited the midwives' return. They all pressed into the small space, eager to hear what happened in the royal court. Shiphrah spilled the king's secret plan—to kill all the baby boys upon delivery.[9]

"But how?" one woman gasped.

"He knows we're the first ones to see the child exit the birth canal, the first to know the sex of the baby. If it is a boy, he wants us to kill it without anyone noticing."

"Even the mother?" one interjected.

"Especially the mother," Shiphrah said. "Even he knows that mothers won't suffer the murder of their sons quietly . . . and he wants this all done quietly."

"And what if it is a girl?" another asked.

"The instruction is to let the girls live," Puah answered.

The horror of it all hushed the room. One of the midwives, herself pregnant, cradled her belly. "I had hoped for a son, but now . . ." Her whisper trailed off into tears. Within seconds she disappeared into the embrace of the women beside her, crying together the tears of the inconsolable.

"We have a secret plan of our own," Shiphrah announced. "We will do as our mothers and their mothers have done— deliver babies."

"We are the strong arms and soft hands of God, and we cannot do otherwise," Puah added.

The unanimous agreement meant that the women had just organized their first act of civil disobedience.[10] They would defy Pharaoh with every delivery. Every refusal to look and discriminate based on gender became an act of holy defiance. Their resistance would be looking on each child with the eyes of God—not the eyes of Pharaoh.

It is a good thing that the women were skilled and organized. Defying Pharaoh required all their education and energy, all the strength and stamina they could muster, as the Hebrew women kept conceiving and birthing babies. At present, the midwives waged their rebellion silently, with no one else the wiser. They didn't want to worry the pregnant women of Goshen. These unlikely rebels did what others never considered— defied Pharaoh in a sustained campaign for who knows how long—in order to protect life. They let the boys live. For a long time Pharaoh didn't even know he was losing.

◆   ◆   ◆

Rosa Parks grew up watching buses. She would watch the school bus come for the white students and take them to nice schools while she walked to an under-resourced school with the other black students. She grew up aware of racism, so evident in the Jim Crow laws of the South. And while she was quiet, she was never one to accept discrimination.

She joined the local chapter of the NAACP (National Association for the Advancement of Colored People) in 1943 and became its secretary, the only position offered to her as a woman. The next year she investigated the case of Recy Taylor, a young black woman who was gang-raped on her way home from church one Sunday morning. Recy refused to remain silent about her kidnapping and rape at the hands of six white men, and Rosa joined her in voicing outrage and organizing a community response to attract attention to the violent injustice.

About ten years later, Emmett Till, a fourteen-year-old black boy, was lynched in Mississippi. The black community could not look away, nor could they be consoled at such a brutal loss. Rosa said that Emmett was on her mind that day in December 1955 when she sat on the bus after a long day's work. She was tired, she said, not from work but from the weight of racism that oppressed her community. So when she was asked to move to the back of the bus to make room for white passengers, she refused. She moved over toward the window, allowing room for a passenger to easily sit next to her, but she wouldn't go to the back of the bus like a second-class citizen. She—and Recy and Emmett—deserved better.

The bus driver threatened to call the police and have her arrested for her refusal to move. "You may do that," she said. It wasn't only her years working at the NAACP that prepared her for that day. Earlier that very year she had attended the Highlander Folk School in Tennessee, a center that trained young and emerging activists. She sat under the teaching of Septima Clark, a director at the school as well as a credentialed professor. Septima equipped Rosa with knowledge and mentored her in the ways of social justice in the face of racism. Rosa was ready for resistance before she ever got on that bus.

Rosa's Thursday evening arrest was a catalyst for the black community. Within days, community organizers decided on a bus boycott to coincide with Rosa's trial, set for the following Monday. So on Sunday morning local black churches had flyers announcing the boycott to congregants. On Sunday evening there was a rally held at the Mt. Zion AME Zion Church, where a young preacher, Martin Luther King Jr., was given the pulpit for one of his first political speeches. He encouraged the congregation to boycott the buses all day on Monday in solidarity with Rosa as she stood trial.

What is often missed in the history is that Rosa wasn't the first to refuse to give up her seat on the bus. Before her came Irene Morgan, Lillie Mae Bradford, Sarah Louise Keys, Claudette Colvin, Aurelia Browder, Susie McDonald, and others.

But Rosa was the match. The black community boycotted the buses for 381 days, until the Supreme Court ruled in favor of some of the above-named women, resulting in the repeal of the segregated bus laws in Montgomery and other southern cities. Many of the women involved in organizing the boycott over those many months were also trained by Septima Clark, whom Martin Luther King Jr. called "the mother of the movement." Many women preceded Rosa and stood with her when her time came to defy the pharaonic forces of segregation and racism. They were ready to resist.

Can you imagine going to church on Sunday morning and finding a flyer in your bulletin about a bus boycott on Monday? Or going to the Sunday evening service and watching it transform into an organizing rally to reveal injustices in the city that impact your community? And can you see the preacher in the pulpit? He talks about biblical justice and mobilizing the church to be the church on Monday—defying Pharaoh. It takes my breath away to envision such a congregation. But in those pews were good women trained and ready to resist, women who feared God. They remind me of Shiphrah, Puah, and the other midwives. And though we haven't spoken of Miriam yet, Septima Clark bears a resemblance to her, as both women paved the way for men who would join the liberation ranks— Moses and Martin Luther King Jr. The women were fired up and ready to go!

•   •   •

Pharaoh underestimated the women. He never thought it possible that anyone would disobey his order. He certainly couldn't imagine *women* thwarting his operation. But at some point—the story does not say when or how—he realized that baby boys continued to be delivered in Goshen.

Shiphrah and Puah stood before the king a second time, more tense than before. "Why have you done this, and allowed the boys to live?"[11] The midwives responded, "Because the Hebrew women are not like the Egyptian women; for they are vigorous and give birth before the midwife comes to them."[12] The clever women used Pharaoh's prejudice against him. Yes, Hebrew and Egyptian women are different. Our women, like insects, spit out their young so fast. By the time we arrive, they not only have given birth but also have seen the child and know too much. We couldn't carry out your plan even if we wanted to, sir. They looked Pharaoh in the eye—and lied.

The next thing we learn isn't how Pharaoh deals with them but how God responds. God blesses them and the other Hebrews with families, allowing them to continue to be fruitful and multiply despite the genocidal climate. Maybe the author of Proverbs had Shiphrah and Puah in mind when he wrote, "In the fear of the LORD one has strong confidence, and one's children will have a refuge. The fear of the LORD is a fountain of life, so that one may avoid the snares of death."[13] Those who fear God usher in life—even or especially in the face of death.

Many Christians say we are meant to obey the government at all times and in all things. Romans 13 is often cited, as if it were a universal statement on citizenship and governments. But Paul, apostle that he was, still wrote as a citizen of Rome, a man in a patriarchal world, someone educated and therefore possessing a measure of privilege not afforded most, certainly not the Hebrew women along the Nile River.[14] In this seminal incident in Exodus, we see that fearing God can look like lying to the powers that sponsor death. Fearing God requires acute discernment, mastery of wits, and some subversive strength. It is possessing the nerve to stand up to the pharaohs of our day and their policies that promote death: their refusal to offer sanctuary to refugees fleeing conflict zones; their attempt to withhold health care from children living under the poverty line; their expansion of private prisons that feed on men of color at high rates and rob them of years with their family and community.

Sometimes we defy the state to demonstrate its error, to show its ignorance, or to unmask its deeper intent. I remember Lisa Sharon Harper, public theologian and activist, standing on the Supreme Court steps to decry the death penalty with others, accepting arrest to show the immorality of the law. I remember more recently, in June 2018, the thousand or so women who marched in Washington, DC, and staged a sit-in at the Senate building to protest the zero-tolerance immigration policy that separated children from their parents at our border. They declared, "Women disobey!" And I watched as 630 of them got arrested to bring attention to the administration's horrific policy toward families fleeing harm. I remember one morning the previous June turning on the television to see a black woman, Bree Newsome, shinnying up a flagpole in South Carolina. She took down the Confederate flag, a symbol of racial terrorism to African Americans, from the statehouse grounds. As she came down to face arrest for her brazen act of civil disobedience, she recited Psalm 23. She would fear no evil.

A filmmaker and an activist, Bree said she had the Charleston massacre on her mind, in which a white supremacist entered an evening Bible study at Mother Emanuel, as the AME church was called, and killed nine African Americans. The historic church was a hub for community organizing and kept the tradition of standing for civil rights. The wound to the community cut deep, as the loss was so personal. This triggered many sleepless nights for Bree, and ten days later she was pushing back against the racial terrorism as she dethroned its symbol from the South Carolina State House. It took less than forty-five minutes for someone to raise the flag again, but Bree had already captured the imagination of a nation. She made us see the violence connected to that flag and see the root of the terror in our own soil.

It is striking that for these women, real death or its threat was the catalyst for their defiance. Bree Newsome carried the fresh memory of those gunned down in the Charleston massacre, and Rosa Parks held the memory of young Emmett Till lynched in Mississippi. The women in Washington, DC, thought of the children separated in detention centers, whose cries for their mothers they heard on an audio recording. Perhaps Shiphrah thought of the boy she just delivered in the dark morning hours before the sun woke, and Puah thought of her neighbor on the verge of labor with her first child. They stood on the threshold of life and death and knew that as God-fearing women, the only thing they could do was choose life, even if it meant defying Pharaoh. Walter Brueggemann says that what counts in this story is "that the Hebrew mothers are invested with dangerous, liberated power for life which no one can deter."[15]

•　　　•　　　•

Early in Exodus we see the king with his own amnesia, assumptions, and anxieties, which he almost immediately parlays into state policy, conscripting the Israelites to build storehouses for him. In Exodus 1:11, the narrator refers to the king as *Pharaoh*, an Egyptian title that translates as "The Great House"[16] (think "White House," "City Hall," or "The Regime"). It is a first in the story, the king being called Pharaoh, and it suggests that the desires of the individual ruler have now blended with the state apparatus. Pharaoh garners support for his enslavement policy by playing upon the insecurities of the Egyptian citizens, who are fearful of surrounding nations coming back to conquer them. The Israelites are a security risk, Pharaoh tells his people, as they could rise up to aid Egypt's foreign enemies. (National security has long been an effective wedge issue.) Now when the everyday Egyptians saw the fruitfulness of the neighboring Israelites, they dreaded them like the king did.[17] They might have already been wary of the delta community, as poverty can breed jealousy and resentment—but it appears that the king and his administration empowered any negative sentiments they harbored about the Hebrews, employing their own strategy to divide the people.

This subtle progression from private to national interest happens again in the king's interactions with the midwives. The king has his own plan to curb the high birth rates of the people who trouble him. He tries to implement his covert plan but fails. And so he turns to a state-sponsored solution. Now he counts on the support of the Egyptian population, who share his dread, to carry out a campaign against the Hebrews. He is known as Pharaoh from here on out in the narrative because his own personal program is now owned by the state apparatus and condoned by the masses. The king's wishes and the regime's agenda are now one and the same—thus, pharaonic, of "The Great House."

Pharaoh boldly involved all Egyptians in his death edict: "Then Pharaoh commanded all his people, 'Every boy that is born to the Hebrews you shall throw into the Nile, but you shall let every girl live.'"[18] Pharaoh's functionaries carried out the initiative for the most part, but all were expected to support it. Death to newborn Hebrew males became state policy and the new normal, and this was how Pharaoh made all Egyptians complicit.[19]

•   •   •

Under apartheid in South Africa, the government oppressed people of color. Forced removals left them living in townships or other undesirable neighborhoods, and education policy dictated that all children attend segregated schools. If black men wished to work outside the township, they were required to carry passbooks to demonstrate they had permission to enter the city. There was no doubting the disdain the government had for these communities of color.

These various policies not only harmed one community but also benefited another. The whites of South Africa, be they Afrikaner or English, were still able to purchase and own land. They could access the best education and get advanced degrees leading to higher-paying jobs. As a matter of fact, they had the advantage of less competition for land, housing, education, jobs, and so on. The apartheid state was such that whites didn't even have to see the townships and their dire conditions from their own neighborhoods. The separation by skin color made all white South Africans beneficiaries.

The whites' innocent comings to and from school and the (whites-only) beaches and churches looked normal. They weren't hurting anyone. Maybe the government was harsh on people of color, but that was its business. After all, the government was just trying to keep the races separate to keep the peace. But the whites' daily involvement in the apartheid regime was a mark of complicity. They didn't want their lives disrupted, so they allowed the regime to carry on. This is how complicity works—it feels benign in a good neighborhood, but the townships know it's malignant and it's killing them.

My first visit to South Africa in 2009 opened my eyes to what systemic racism looks like, how it operates, and how its legacy lasts long after the dismantling of the apartheid state. I learned about perpetrators and beneficiaries, concepts new to my vocabulary, as I watched how whiteness worked in the past and continues to work in the present. But my education didn't end on the wine farms of Stellenbosch, on the beaches of Cape Town, on Robben Island, or when I boarded my flight in Johannesburg. I returned to the United States with fresh eyes.

Once stateside, I began to see how racism functions in my own country. I saw beyond simple caricatures of a name-calling white person or a coworker telling an obviously racist joke. I began to discern patterns of treatment that have continued since slavery and Jim Crow laws were abolished. Even the monumental civil rights movement had not erased the stain and ongoing realities of systemic racism in America. Homeownership, education options, job opportunities, and even maternal mortality rates are different for black people—statistics and stories point to these truths.

The enslavement of black people began as an economic strategy for a young nation in need of free labor. Slavery calibrated the economy for white communities to flourish without regard for black bodies. That legacy continues today. It's easy to name the perpetrators: the ones who crafted the slave system that dominated the South, slave traders and slave-owning families; government men like Governor George Wallace and the police who carried out his orders on the Edmund Pettus Bridge in Selma, Alabama; the lynch mobs and the racist zealots burning crosses while cloaked in white. Harder was adding my name to the list, not as a perpetrator but as a beneficiary of the racist systems that still shape our society.

Throughout my life, I've had more doors open to me because I'm not black. Yes, my father worked hard in school and built his own business. "Nothing was ever handed to me," he says. Yet he and his father and his father's father had the advantage of being white, which empowered their work in incalculable ways. I am his direct beneficiary. That is, I am heir to my father's hard work—and any advantage he had because he wasn't black when he enrolled in college, applied for a business loan, and bid on a home in a nice middle-class neighborhood.

Just like the legacy of slavery lingers down the generations, so too the accrued advantages of whiteness. My country has oppressed black families, and modern pharaohs have made me complicit.

•   •   •

The women of Egypt were made complicit in their pharaoh's targeted infanticide. Many lived away from the royal house and out of earshot of the imperial edicts; maybe they didn't know—yet. But others would have heard. Did they nod in agreement, sharing Pharaoh's disdain for the Hebrews? Did they think nothing of the decree and so just go about their business? Or were some troubled early on? For now, all we know is that the daughters of Egypt are implicated, though silent.

The Hebrew women continue to conceive, carry, and give birth to sons and daughters in Goshen. Even Shiphrah's belly swells with new life as she brings other babies into the world.

Puah mothers the midwives, encouraging them to keep delivering children as they come. "Fear God only," she exhorts.

These women demonstrate deliverance not as warriors on the battlefield but as midwives at the birthing stool, bringing life into a dangerous world. They refuse to fear Pharaoh and save many lives. Wilda Gafney rightly calls Shiphrah and Puah "the first deliverers in the book of deliverance."[20] Perhaps their role in the Exodus story ignited the imagination of the psalmist, allowing him to see that sometimes God delivers like a midwife—and so he sings of God "who took me from the womb" and "kept me safe on my mother's breast" and who surrounds him with comfort.[21] In a contemporary voice, Juliana Claassens notes, "The metaphor of God as Midwife attests to the fact that God is resolutely on the side of life, working hard to allow new life to enter this world."[22] This is another gift from Shiphrah and Puah—the ability to see God with feminine hands in the work of shalom and salvation.

The midwives fear God in active ways—and this includes defying Pharaoh. In their hierarchy of fears, it is God who most energizes them toward obedience amid dangerous times. Marshaling all their skill, they organize against death. They demonstrate a nervy faith that challenges us to do the same. Where do we see death and discrimination in our communities? Do we fear God in such a way that we are willing to defy pharaonic policies that threaten the lives of sons—and daughters?

"Let the girls live," Pharaoh said. It would be the beginning of his downfall—underestimating the women. The midwives are the first in a succession of defiance. Unfortunately, their resistance succeeds for only a brief time, as Pharaoh's public edict empowers all of Egypt to kill the next generation of boys. But still the midwives persist. The movement into freedom takes time and requires our stamina even when the evidence of our success wanes. Rosa Parks's case languished in the courts, and the Confederate flag was raised less than an hour after Bree Newsome took it down. We don't know how long it will take before we see freedom's shore, but we will settle for nothing less than shalom for all. Since we always fear God, we always resist Pharaoh.

Chapter 3

JOCHEBED

Freedom through Relinquishment

Jochebed was raised by the reeds of the Nile Delta. The tall, bending grasses of the river surrounded her like a cocoon, shading her from the sun and the gaze of the Egyptians alike. She discovered early that a good thicket of reeds offers a shelter, a place to hide from chores and other harsh realities. The supple green strands held her stories and rustled to the rhythm of her songs. She liked digging her toes into the cool, wet soil, tangling with the roots. Tucked into the thicket, she felt safe. But soon enough the breeze changed direction, and she was revealed until the next time.

Once a woman, Jochebed married, conceived, and gave birth to a son. This daughter of Levi married a man from the Levite house—a proper match for a good daughter. But this good woman bore a son at a very bad time. The family fortunes had been dwindling for some time.[1] Her father, Levi,[2] came to Egypt when his brother Joseph was still alive, when he was the food czar over the land. But then this pharaoh, with no memory of those days, rose to power. Over time their family showed the loss—premature deaths, no income, no time to cultivate crops or to create businesses to support their needs. Then came the harshest blow: the death edict for their sons. Jochebed watched as her world slowly changed, and never for the better.

Still, she married. Pharaoh cannot take everything, try as he might. What the narrator does not mention here is that Jochebed already had a son and a daughter, both born before the edict. They were her solace, her sun and moon. When she learned she was pregnant again, it hit her like . . . a ton of bricks, she confessed. This one would be hard labor; she knew it in her bones.

Our narrator fast-forwards through the months of unknowing (does she carry a boy or a girl, life or death?) to the arrival of her son. "When she saw that he was a fine baby, she hid him for three months."[3] She recognizes that her boy is good, using the very same word God uses in describing the days of creation.[4] Jochebed's son possessed the deep goodness of creation, stamped with God's own image, a boy as good as anything God ever made. Her eyes might have been tired and full of tears, but she saw clearly.

It might be that after the flood of bad news coming from the royal regime, the narrator wants us to hear that in the shadow of the brickyards, life still happened. Pharaoh's word couldn't undercut God's word spoken at the beginning. And what's more, a new creation was underway. Goodness entered the world again and, like yeast, would do its slow, steady work of transformation, expansion. Maybe we are meant to see that hope is on the way, that the world will be recalibrated toward original shalom soon enough.

Jochebed, whose name we learn later in the book of Exodus, birthed life under a death order.[5] As commonplace as that might seem, don't miss the act of defiance her pregnancy was under such conditions. The resistance of the midwives continued and expanded as the Hebrew women, along with all of Egypt, knew the order yet continued to conceive, birth, and deliver boys. They did so at immense risk.[6]

•   •   •

Kallie Wood is a Nakoda Cree from Moose Jaw, Saskatchewan. She is a twin. Her mother was still in the birthing suite, exhausted from delivering her daughters, when an "Indian agent" appointed by the Canadian government walked into the room and took both her babies. She never saw them again. She left the hospital empty-handed. The infants were put up for adoption by the government. Kallie was separated from her mother and her twin sister that day. A non-Indigenous family adopted her and raised her with much love. But she grew up without knowledge of her Indigenous heritage, without connection to her tribe or birth family.[7] Kallie is a survivor of the Sixties Scoop, affecting approximately twenty thousand children from the 1950s to 1980s across Canada. Similar programs were implemented in Australia, targeting Aboriginal families, and in the United States, targeting Native American families.[8] Survivors suffer ongoing trauma that reaches into subsequent generations, and they call the government policies nothing short of cultural genocide.[9]

Indigenous women the world over know the risk of giving birth under the banner of one empire or another, the way colonization threatens the fabric of their families. Children routinely separated from their mothers are sent to faraway residential schools or, as in Kallie's case, are adopted right out of their mother's arms. Slavery in America separated families too.

Sadly, our country has not stopped the practice of family separation, as the world witnessed when we ignored any semblance of human rights (or human decency) at our southern border as recently as 2018. Mothers and their children continue to be at risk, subject to the pharaonic powers of our day.

•   •   •

Birth is dangerous for mother and child in Burundi too. The maternal and infant mortality rates across the country are dire. When my husband and I began working in Bubanza, about forty-five minutes north of the capital city, there were so many tiny coffins. Every week a funeral procession wove around the thatch huts to the makeshift cemetery. Loss was a constant in the community. Sometimes even the mother did not survive the birth.

We partnered with 660 Batwa families who lived in Bubanza to secure national identity cards for all the adults to ensure they had citizenship, protection under the law, and access to basic health care. But the incessant burial of small coffins beat against my husband's heart. We decided to fast-track birth certificates for the youngest and most vulnerable babies so that they could access the local government health clinic. We made sure the women got identity cards first so that as mothers, they could take advantage of prenatal care and maybe even assistance with deliveries.

But the local clinic was not enough. It was understaffed and often out of necessary medicines and supplies. So through Communities of Hope (my and Claude's Burundian NGO) and in partnership with Community of Faith in Cypress, Texas, we opened a small health center with one nurse, Lydia, which was attached to the elementary school we had established. Lydia served the children, but she also received pregnant women and gave them instructions on prenatal health and other support. Soon after, we began a feeding program for the schoolchildren: fortified porridge in the morning and a hot lunch of beans and vegetables. The mamas-to-be and nursing mothers were included in this program, because lack of nutritious food is a contributing factor to poor maternal health. These simple things—check-ups, daily porridge, and health coaching—went on for years. It was so little, but it was all we could offer.

One morning Lydia was sitting in my office going over the medical reports for the quarter. "No babies died this quarter. Every mother survived the birth."

"Good news," I said. Then I watched her flip through her reports.

"No babies have died in the last twelve months . . . no mothers have been lost, either."

I asked her to check the reports again. Then we began to cry—our first full year where every baby and every mother survived! It took us five years to see a substantial victory over infant and maternal mortality rates. Together we worked to promote life against the pharaonic injustices that beset the poor: marginalization, food insecurity, and lack of health care. Now the Bubanza community needs more birthday candles and fewer coffins. But this is one village among thousands throughout the country. Birth is still too hard for too many.

Women across Burundi and women of color throughout the United States are not the only ones in peril when pregnant. Remember the women fleeing conflict zones in Congo and Sudan. Consider the women of Syria and Iraq who escape regimes with the added weight of a pregnancy, crossing land and sea toward a hoped-for safety. Pregnancy and birth remain precarious—even after the delivery, life remains chock-full of injustice. For too many women the world over, conceiving and bearing children is dangerous work. It might even be the most ordinary kind of defiance in the face of death. The threat overshadowing the Egyptian brickyards in Exodus continues to loom large over our contemporary landscape.

People often ask why, under such conditions, women keep having children. Why don't they stop and stem the tide of risk? The answer, at least in Burundi, isn't singular. In rural communities, the night comes early and lasts long without any electricity to light most homes. Sex is the activity that is available to husbands and wives. It is an opportunity to connect with someone amid daily hardship, a bit of joy to savor when all else is bitter. (While this isn't the entire sexual landscape, it describes many Burundian families.)

But the deeper answer has to do with Burundian culture and survival. Children are not only a blessing; they are an investment in the future, the ones who will care for you in your old age. In a country that struggles to exist due to years of civil war, extreme poverty, and chronic malnourishment, not all children survive into adulthood. So the math is straightforward—you have more children in the hope that some will live, succeed, and care for you. My own mother- and father-in-law birthed ten children and have buried their three eldest sons already, not to count the miscarriages they suffered. But by God's grace, three sons and four daughters are alive to assist them into their twilight years.

Children insure your future in tangible ways. Each baby born is a sign of hope for the family. So you keep having babies, casting bread upon the waters. You never know what harsh weather will come or from what direction—you just hope seed survives with enough to harvest when you are hungry.[10] So it is with children born under duress. They are your hope against the darkness.

Maybe there isn't much of a difference between defiance and hope. To carry on and walk through the valley of the shadow of death is an audacious act of hope. So women continue to marry, conceive, and birth babies. If these women are at all like the Israelites, they increase despite the empire's attempts to quash them. These women say no to every final solution devised by every pharaoh.[11] The women, like Jochebed, embody hope.

Jochebed isn't alone, nor is her situation unique or even rare. It is all too common for women to still find birth an enormous risk, an act of defiance and hope. But hope is not enough. What we witness in Jochebed is how risk becomes the mother of subversive strategies to save her son.

●　　　●　　　●

From the moment of her little boy's birth, Jochebed felt the sand running through the hourglass. She determined right then to hide him. How long would she get to hold him? Long enough to discern his name and to memorize the shape of his cheeks and dimpled chin? For the time being she would call him *matoki*, because he was her "sweet one."[12] She determined to make the most of every minute.

Jesus tells a parable of another woman who hides a good thing: "The kingdom of heaven is like yeast that a woman took and mixed in with three measures of flour until all of it was leavened."[13] The word *mixed* is often translated *hid*. The Greek word in the original text is *enkrypto*, "encrypted," which carries the possible meaning of "secret-code making."[14] This woman hides the yeast. Her subversive handiwork is setting something good in motion.

In the ancient world, leavened bread was made not with the active dry or instant yeasts commercially produced today but with wild yeast, cultivated using a sourdough starter, a mix of flour and water that's fed each day and left to ferment. So the woman in the parable tears off a piece of her sourdough starter (we don't know how much) and hides it in flour. Three measures, or about sixty pounds, of flour. That is a lot of flour. Then she sits out in the full morning sun mixing the two together, adding more water and kneading the mass in full view of her neighbors.

No one notices that she is coding abundance into the dough. It looks like she is making daily bread, enough for her family under Roman occupation. But she keeps kneading. Once the dough is smooth and stretchy, she divides it into bowls. She covers each bowl with a light cloth and lets the dough rest in the warm corners of her courtyard. Slowly the dough begins to rise under cover of the gauze-like cloths. While she busies herself with other household chores, the leaven works quietly.

Hours later when she returns, what was once hidden is revealed. She takes the many risen masses of dough and bakes them. Unbeknownst to anyone, she has made an abundance of bread—enough to feed the neighbors. She fills her basket with the warm loaves and covers them with a cloth. She walks down the street and hands small loaves to the begging children. She tucks a couple of loaves into the empty baskets of the widows wandering the market, trying to determine how to spend the too little they have. She visits a few families she knows are struggling, giving them bread and some dried fruits she purchased with the coins she could spare. She makes multiple trips, each time with more bread for more hungry neighbors.

But why the "hiding" of the yeast if all she's doing is making some extra bread? Perhaps the secret was her redistribution of family resources. Maybe she noticed her neighbors' need and took matters into her own hands, not asking anyone for permission. Eventually her intentions would be revealed. She made enough bread to feed a crowd—with leftovers, even. The hyperbole in operation is key for parables, stretching our imagination. One woman, many loaves. One son saved from the Nile revealed to be the future liberator of an entire nation.

The woman bakes a bounty of bread not to hoard for her own family but to share with the neighborhood. She distributes the bread to the hungry like a true disciple of Jesus. At least this is what I imagine she did with the hidden yeast. She hid yeast for a short time, revealing loaves to be shared later. Jesus didn't say this was women's work but, rather, the kingdom at work in the woman's able hands.

In the next two chapters in Matthew's Gospel, he will tell us about how Jesus multiplied bread, feeding five thousand and then four thousand on another occasion.[15] We will see Jesus tell his disciples to hand out the bread to the hungry—to share in the bread business, as it were. But the woman in the parable intuitively knows about hidden work and how to feed the hungry by multiplying her daily yield with her own two holy hands.

◆   ◆   ◆

Mama Rose, like the mothers before her, was clever when it came to stretching provisions for her growing family. When her husband gave her grocery money, she went to the market to buy beans, cassava, some fruits, and charcoal. But she tucked away some money in an empty Nido can that she hid under her bed. This was her habit. Sometimes her husband came home with a chicken or a bunch of green bananas and a few mangoes, since people occasionally paid pastors in kind instead of in cash. Every few months, though, he came home empty-handed: no money, no meat, no mangoes. But dinnertime would come, and Mama Rose would manage to bring some small thing to the table—maybe only potatoes and a thinned tomato sauce. Her husband would bless the food, thanking God for miraculous provision, and they and their children would gather around the platter and eat. Only years later did my husband, Claude, learn that his mother hid money away every week so she could buy food on those empty-handed days.

Hiding isn't always bad. As the stories of Mama Rose and the woman who hides the yeast reveal, it is a strategy for protecting and providing. Think of other instances: Bibles smuggled into China to the network of clandestine house churches, missionaries disguised as mere ESL teachers to carry the gospel into Asia, the Underground Railroad during the antebellum period and the coded language of the spirituals, even hiding places for Jewish families in attics and behind walls in neighbors' homes. We learn from these examples that hiding is a time-honored skill in the resistance against death edicts, persecution, and all other kinds of injustice.

●　　　　●　　　　●

In 2017 I traveled to Israel-Palestine with a group of women to meet the peacemakers in the region. On our first day together we visited Yad Vashem, the World Holocaust Remembrance Center in Jerusalem. Our tour guide was a short, stout woman with long, dark hair and a heavy British accent. As we fiddled with headsets handed to us for the tour, she introduced herself and led us to a long double colonnade of trees. "These trees," she began, "represent the Righteous Among the Nations." Each tree was planted in honor of a non-Jewish person who took the risk to save Jewish people during the Holocaust. As we were a group of Americans, she took us to the tree that honored Oskar and Emilie Schindler of *Schindler's List* fame. She was confident, and correct, that we'd recognize Oskar's name. He is among the righteous remembered for his efforts to save over thirteen hundred Jews. "Don't forget Emilie; her name is there for a reason," our guide reminded us. "She might even have been the first of the two to begin the righteous work," she said with a raised brow just before she turned on her heels and led us down into the museum.

I took note, scribbling Emilie's name in the margin of my journal that night. Months later, when I returned to the States, I learned that Emilie Schindler had written her own memoir. She begins by stating clearly that Oskar wasn't a hero—and neither was she: "we only did what we had to do."[16] While she pushes against the hero narrative from the first page, she also claims her own place in the story of rescue.

As the Nazi campaign became more widespread and their agenda more evident, Emilie felt a deep fear she could not shake. The more the regime spoke of the glorious destiny of Germany, the more she worried. She tried to warn Oskar repeatedly, but he wasn't listening; he was only trying to survive. Eventually someone well placed in the regime offered Oskar the chance to run an enamelware factory previously owned by Jewish industrialists. This would bring them in close proximity to Jewish workers and their plight.[17]

We know from watching *Schindler's List* what Oskar did next. He ran the factory with Jewish workers from the nearby Plaschow camp. He did what he could to bargain for their safety as the war carried on. When word came that the Germans were closing the camp and planned to send all Jews, including his workers, to Auschwitz, he came up with another plan. While his Jewish workers created the infamous list of people to save, he tried to secure a munitions factory to transfer the workers and save them from a certain death.

What was lost on the cutting-room floor of the big-budget film is the work of Emilie. It was Emilie who negotiated for the necessary permit for the munitions factory when her husband was at his wits' end. It was Emilie who bartered on the black market to get medicine and food for the Jews in the factory, who operated a feeding program and hand-fed the weakest, who arranged for burials in a Catholic cemetery to protect their bodies from the ovens. She saved an additional 250 Jewish men and women from a Polish mine by agreeing to absorb them into the factory and overseeing the clandestine transfer herself.

Emilie paints a portrait of Oskar as a man whose fortitude frayed during the waning years of the war. He spent most of his time in Kracow, miles away, while she ran the munitions factory almost entirely by herself. And yet she did have some help. When the train car with all the Jewish women was misdirected to Auschwitz, it was a family friend, Hilde, who used her cunning (and maybe her feminine charm, Emilie adds) to retrieve the women and see them safely delivered to the factory. When food rations dwindled, Emilie brokered a deal with a German aristocrat, Frau von Daubek, owner of a mill, to get grain for her workers. Other women took risks alongside her.

Emilie writes that the munitions factory never produced a single bullet. The factory was meant to be a refuge for Jews.[18] She hid the Jews in plain sight, under the facade of a factory, to ensure their safety until the end of the war. She and Oskar spared the lives of over thirteen hundred Jewish people. When *Schindler's List* debuted in movie theaters, Emilie's contribution was ignored. But what is hidden will be revealed in due time.

The Yad Vashem memorial names many other women among the righteous, calling them "Women of Valor" in accordance with Proverbs 31. The majority were ordinary women who, amid pharaonic times, knew that hiding was required of them. They hid Jews in their homes and churches, they hid Jewish identities by offering falsified documents, they smuggled Jews across borders to safety. These women embody the culminating words of the proverb "Charm is deceitful, and beauty is vain, but a woman who fears the LORD is to be praised."[19]

•   •   •

Hiding her child afforded Jochebed time. Three months was as long as she could keep him hidden from the unjust world of Pharaoh, his soldiers, and the Egyptian zealots his agenda empowered. Three months—her only defense against the everyday Egyptians, who remained silent while small bodies floated down the river.

She nursed him with breast milk and tears. She sang him lullabies of horses and chariots being tossed into the sea, girls dancing under the golden moon, and little boys running free along the shores of the Nile without fear. In the early mornings while the world was still, Jochebed studied the river, returning to the reeds. The speeding currents, the ever-hungry crocodiles, and the jagged edges of the riverbank as it turned out of sight—this would be *matoki*'s final fate. And as she watched the waterline those three months, she saw someone.

She stood tall and slender against the morning light. She moved with the poise and freedom of a royal daughter. She often walked the shoreline accompanied by her handmaids—but not always. "Oh to be rich and royal," Jochebed sighed, "to conceive and birth children, to watch them grow." All the forced Hebrew labor in the brickyards benefited women like her. No harm comes to a royal.

And yet, she seemed different. Other bejeweled women frolicked in the sunlight, their laughter drowning out all birdsong. But this woman was pensive. She'd submerge her body in the water, surrendering as if it were a ritual cleansing.

Their eyes locked once, across the river and through the reeds. The woman did not look away or look through Jochebed. It was their first meeting. There was a stirring in the house. Jochebed turned and made her way to her *matoki*, who was growing harder to hide and to hush. As she pulled him to her breast, she thought about the woman. Was she imagining things? Was the woman like all the other royals? Or could her intentions be different than Pharaoh's?

Jochebed woke in the middle of the night. As she whispered moonlight prayers to a God who seemed to have forgotten her, an audacious idea emerged.

•   •   •

Since she could hide him no longer, it was time for another risk. Jochebed hunted for a basket with the tightest weave she could find, then carefully sealed the gaps with bitumen and pitch.

While the makeshift raft dried in the sun, I imagine she looked across the river one more time, wondering about the woman and if she could really be trusted.

She carefully put her *matoki* in the waterproof basket. It was an ark of sorts, according to the narrator, one meant to save this child from another unstoppable flood. Salvation for him would mean relinquishment for her.[20]

The next thing we're told is that she put the boy and basket in the reeds on the bank of the Nile. I had assumed she launched her son across the river in the hope that he would make it safely over. But there is another way to read this story: Jochebed guided the basket across the river herself and put it in the thicket of reeds on purpose. She took on the danger of negotiating the waters, ensuring that neither Leviathan nor Pharaoh would claim her boy's life. This sounds like the mothers I know.

Putting the boy in the reeds would ensure that the Nile's currents didn't carry him downstream.[21] But it also meant he'd be strategically in view of the palace, where Jochebed knew the woman could find him. Jochebed was betting on the woman's humanity, hoping she wasn't like the others who seemed indifferent to the death edict.

◆   ◆   ◆

As I watch Jochebed put her son in the reeds, I'm haunted by Hagar, another grieving mother.

Hagar, given as a slave to Sarah and then as a wife to Abraham, conceived and gave birth to a son. While the arrival of Ishmael was meant to solve the problem of Sarah's barrenness, it only complicated matters and made Hagar's affliction more severe.[22] Hagar escaped early on, returned under divine order, but was finally cast out by Abraham with a paltry bit of bread and a skin of water.

Once the provisions were gone, things in the wilderness turned dire. Hagar took her son and *put* him under a bush to shade him from the piercing sun. She sat nearby, expecting his imminent death. This is the vocabulary of burial.[23] It is the same verb in Hebrew used to describe how Jochebed *put* her boy in a raft and then *put* him in the reeds. Was she preparing him for life or death? Given the risk involved in her actions, maybe she was unsure what fate awaited her son. This was a true risk with no guarantees.

We hear Hagar's plaintive cry, "Do not let me look on the death of my child."[24] Words like this must have been on the lips of Jochebed as she swam back to the other side of the river and watched from afar. The Lord spared Ishmael; will he spare this unnamed son?

•   •   •

Under apartheid in South Africa, it was illegal for a white person to have sex with a black person, according to the Immorality Act of 1927. If caught, you could face up to five years in prison—at least that was the penalty for black people. So when Patricia Nombuyiselo Noah gave birth to her son, he was evidence of her crime. With a white father and a black mother, her boy was light-skinned and at risk from the very beginning. When Patricia delivered him, the hospital staff was required to report the child, to report her crime. When asked about the father, she lied, saying he was from Swaziland. She lied again on her son's birth certificate, saying the father was born in KaNgwane, a semi-sovereign region for Swazi people living in South Africa. It was the only way to protect them both. Had she been reported, her son would have been taken from her and raised in a boarding school with other mixed-race children. So she lied. She hid his identity from the state.

Patricia was a deeply religious woman. She attended three different churches each Sunday. She went to Rhema Bible Church, a mixed church, to participate in the jubilant praise of God. Then she traveled to a wealthy white neighborhood to attend Rosebank Union, where she got a deeper exposition of Scripture. Then she would drive to a black church, usually the Methodist church where her own mother was a member, to experience even further the passion of worship. "I'm here to fill up on my blessings for the week," she'd tell her son. In addition to all that, she would take her son to church four times during the week for prayer meetings and the like. Patricia's faithfulness never waned. And yet this God-fearing woman knew that apartheid was wrong, that the Immorality Act was wrong, and so she lied to the authorities, keeping her son safe by her side.

Trevor Noah laughs now as he tells the story to Oprah, but he remembers his mother telling him to go hide at odd times during his childhood. He thought it was a game she was playing with him, so he would hide under the bed or in a closet. What he learned later from his grandmother was he was told to hide when the police came around. Until apartheid ended, he was under threat.

Trevor's mom employed other tactics to hide his identity. When she wanted to take him to the park, she would invite Queen, a neighbor with lighter brown skin, to join them. Queen and Trevor would walk side by side, and Patricia would walk behind, masquerading as the black nanny. When walking alone with him in the city, if they saw a policeman, she would drop his hand and push him away from her to create the illusion that they weren't together. Even at his grandmother's house in a black township, Trevor stayed cloistered in the family compound to protect him from being taken by the government and the rest of the family from being punished for colluding with Patricia's crime. Hiding Trevor's identity and even presence was part of mothering him until apartheid ended when he was six years old.[25]

I see in Patricia the subversive strength of Jochebed. She gave birth to a mixed son under apartheid, well before Nelson Mandela was released from prison or apartheid's end was on the horizon. She risked much; she strategized more. She lied. She hid her son in the house, disguised their connection in public, and even falsified information on government documents. She navigated risk and protected his life, as God-fearing women did in Exodus and do to this day.

•   •   •

Jochebed conceives and carries a child in an environment fraught with peril. She gives birth with the assistance of midwives and enters into the resistance movement. Already a mother, this is not new to her; she has risked before. Now, however, her portfolio of risk increases as she hides her son from the imperial policy that seeks to kill him, and strategizes to save him by delivering him to the feet of a woman she hopes she can trust. From the moment her son is born, she works to save him with a series of small and significant maneuvers, refusing to give in to the threats, which loom like pyramids.

This is, as Walter Brueggemann notes, a rescue narrative.[26] The focus of the narrator is not on the birth but on the jeopardy of the child. The dangerous conditions for Jochebed on the Hebrew side of the Nile River invite us to consider how this son will be saved from the death edict, if that is even possible. Pharaoh wants us to believe that it is not possible to escape his orders, but the midwives have already shown us that it can be done. Will this mother find another way to subvert Pharaoh?

Her grit is impressive and incessant. She doesn't stop until she exhausts every option to save her boy. He is, after all, her *matoki*. Others see him as evidence of a crime; they call those like him a thug, an animal, an insect, or worse. But mothers know better: each child is a sweet thing worth saving.

Even if it means relinquishment, even if it means entrusting him to another woman—Jochebed stops at nothing, even entrapment, to secure her boy's life. You feel the injustice of it all weighing down on her. And the odds are not in favor of these mothers and midwives pushing against the pharaonic regime. Maybe for a moment we give in to Pharaoh's thinking—these women are no threat, no match for him.

But the deliverance of God is like these women hidden in the Exodus story, often unnamed and unnoticed. Pharaoh did not see them and often we have not—but they are there quietly working liberation one risk at a time. They are birthing, hiding, and even crossing rivers of injustice to deliver children from death. They are forming alliances and trying new ways to enact small salvations.

Chapter 4

BITHIAH

Freedom through Leveraged Privilege

Born into privilege, Pharaoh's daughter was nursed on narratives of Egyptian greatness. She grew up among the elite, watching them parade through the palace with curried favor and attendants. She never lifted a finger and never knew any different. Life was good alongside the Nile River, which seemed to wind and bend to her father's command.

She'd often visit the various balconies of his household and observe the slow rise of the mighty pyramids and storehouses. She marveled at his capacity to erect such feats of architecture. Everything around her father, from the palace pillars that seemed to hold up the sky to the mountain-shaped monuments emerging from the sands, communicated his massive strength and sweeping significance.

When the sun began to descend into the river and the world turned burnt orange with threads of pink, Bithiah[1] sometimes walked the shoreline. She'd slip off her sandals to feel the warm sand and cool water in turn. While she was privileged, she wasn't powerful, so she soaked in simple pleasures afforded her along the river.

One afternoon amid such a walk, a baby washed up, nearly touching her bare feet. A Hebrew boy, mere days old it appeared, drowned and now within arm's reach. The servants ran to grab the child, as if to erase the incident altogether. Royal women weren't supposed to witness the underside of life in the empire.

But they were too late. The waterlogged infant was the evidence she could not deny. As the serpentine river swallowed the sun whole, she came to know that all the rumors were true. Her father had turned the Nile into a watery grave.

In the following weeks, Bithiah kept to herself. She seldom took to the balcony, shunning Pharaoh's demonstration of building prowess and the brutality she knew undergirded it. The monuments and brickyards made her feel small. Even a royal daughter could not stop the death dealing of a king.

She spent a handful of sleepless nights staring out her window, keeping company with the moon. The only sound that broke the midnight silence were the plaintive songs coming from across the river. Laments from bereft mothers carried dark truths from their camp. Bithiah felt complicit in the deathly way of things, and the sad songs gave an odd solace to her troubled spirit. Other than hum along, night after night, what could anyone expect her to do?

One day Pharaoh was marching out to the construction site with a regiment of armed guards to survey the progress firsthand. State counselors were convening in the grand hall to discuss matters of strategy to keep the Hebrews in their place. Servants scurried about, tending to the soldiers, the statesmen, and the royal women lounging in the gardens. No one took notice of the insignificant procession of the young woman and her maids down to the shore.

Bithiah, feeling the weight of her invisibility, disrobed and waded into the water. She engaged in a ritual bathing ceremony of her own design in an attempt to purge the filth of the empire. Something in her broke under the water's surface. Maybe it was mingling in the currents rife with suffering, her pores absorbing the pain—maybe it was a rending that happens when chaos hammers your heart—but she emerged changed. Maybe she was just brokenhearted.[2]

The sun shone like a spotlight on the tall reeds. Just then she noticed a basket bobbing in the waters, shaking the thicket just out of her reach. She waved to her handmaid, instructing her to retrieve the basket. She heard the cry—everything in her ached at the sound. This boy was alive.

•   •   •

Bithiah is not the only one to see small bodies washed ashore. We have seen them too. Wearing a red T-shirt and blue shorts, lying facedown in the sand of a Turkish beach, Alan Kurdi was found dead.[3] He drowned in the Mediterranean Sea as his family tried to escape the civil war in Syria on an overloaded boat captained by smugglers. When the morning sun crossed the coastline, a few locals saw the boy and attempted a rescue. But he was already gone. His lifeless body became a testament to the perils facing refugee families, an image we could not deny.

What could we do? Give to organizations that advocate for refugees? Write our leaders and implore them to support refugee resettlement in the United States? Pray harder in our church services or light candles of remembrance? I did all these things and still felt helpless. Regimes of death dwarf us all, despite our living in enclaves of relative privilege. However, this does not mean we are easily exempt from confronting the injustices that threaten our neighbors, global and otherwise.

We are like Bithiah—privileged yet seemingly powerless, paralyzed. From the outside it appears as if there is only privilege, only complicity. But walking through the palace compound, we find that ease can be punctuated with growing disease. One can be trapped with little or no way to influence the pharaoh. We benefit—and we are bothered.

Initially Bithiah found herself in a closed system of complicity, a pharaonic beneficiary who imagined herself unable to effect any real change. She was one of many royal daughters— and she was not even her father's favorite. But once she began to see the truth, there were decisions to be made.

•   •   •

There is a Jewish tradition that tells of another daughter of another pharaoh—her name is Hagar.[4] When Abraham and Sarah traveled through Egypt, the pharaoh took Sarah, a stunning beauty, as a wife, believing she was the nomad's sister. But Sarah's word caught either his attention or God's, and he realized that she was, in fact, another man's wife.[5] He hastily released her, commanding Abraham to go at once. But, as the story goes, the pharaoh sent his own child as compensation for the misunderstanding. The young, sable-skinned beauty, a prize given by patriarchy, served Sarah. This is how the royal daughter became a slave, an attendant instead of attended to herself.

Did Bithiah grow up hearing Mother Hagar's story spoken among the other royal daughters? Surely they heard within the folds of the telling the ways in which it remained precarious to be Pharaoh's daughter, their birth offering no guarantees.

Hagar is used by men but also by a woman, as Sarah sends in Egypt's daughter to Abraham to provide an heir and erase Sarah's shame as a barren wife. Hagar conceives. In short order the women realize their roles have been reversed, as Pharaoh's daughter carries Abraham's son. Sarah seethes, and then lashes out in waves of mistreatment toward Hagar, proving she is as cruel as she is beautiful. Hagar escapes to the wilderness, encounters a divine manifestation, and is told to return.

Back in the tents of Canaan, Hagar births Ishmael. But instead of the security one would expect for a firstborn son, he is eventually cast out into the wilderness in favor of another heir. Sarah could not tolerate a rival to her own child, birthed amid her advanced age. Hagar and Ishmael, once heirs, now languish under the burning sun. Who would rescue them?

They would have died—had it not been for the appearance of the well. Was it a divine revealing, angelic mercy? Was it due to Mother Hagar's running from place to place, searching with every bit of energy, as some stories say?[6] It certainly wasn't thanks to the help of anyone nearby or that distant woman coddling her son. But Hagar and Ishmael do survive. Years later Mother Hagar finds a wife for Ishmael, and God blesses him with twelve sons, a fruitful nation despite Sarah's attempted sabotage.[7] Among the women of Egypt, Hagar was honored as a survivor rescued from death and obscurity.[8]

I imagine that it was not lost on Bithiah how one woman took advantage of another, concerned solely with her own welfare and that of her son. Her foremother nearly perished, and Sarah did nothing but put her in jeopardy. How could women be so cruel to one another? Why didn't anyone rescue a woman and her child? How could their humanity go unseen? Where was Hagar's ram?[9]

Maybe it needled Bithiah on those long nights overlooking the Nile River, how women were capable of betraying one another. Her Egyptian kinswoman could have been lost forever, so it felt personal. But maybe Bithiah was thinking not only about her tribe but about the larger landscape of womanhood. Sarah could have made another choice. She could have been kind to Hagar and made room for her; she could have spared her and her son. Hagar's humanity could have mattered more to Sarah than her own reputation or progeny. What a stunning testimony that would have been—a woman shunning cultural and patriarchal boundaries to rescue another woman. "Why can't that be our story?" Bithiah might have wondered under the canopy of stars in all their wondrous possibility.

◆   ◆   ◆

"Do you need me to go get a Hebrew woman to nurse your child?" the girl asked. She appeared as if out of the same thicket of reeds as the boy, and her voice brought the awareness that Bithiah was now holding the crying baby. No doubt, he was hungry.

The young Hebrew girl was insistent, wanting to help *her* and *her child*. She saw how the royal woman looked at her baby brother and took to him; she didn't want to miss this opportunity to provide a shelter for him with a sympathetic woman.[10] So before Bithiah could decide otherwise, the clever girl offered a quick solution.

Both women, separated by years and a wide river, knew the heavy truth about where milk could be found. Across the river were women with full breasts but empty arms. Any one of them could nurse this boy she now held. Bithiah wondered if the girl was right—was she his mother now?

She knew the standing order. As an Egyptian, she had no choice but to comply. But resistance rose in her as the baby let out another cry. She knew she stood knee-deep in the rescue operation, in the current of defiance. She looked at the boy, then back at the girl. "Go!" she consented.

•   •   •

When I met Tahany, we were both stateside with our young children. She was wearing her hijab and had two boys clinging to her side. The first day of school overwhelms most of us. We began our conversation with introduction and ease. Time spent in Burundi in proximity to the Muslim community had erased the initial fear and unfamiliarity I had around Islamic women. We became fast friends, always finding each other at pick-up time and visiting while we waited for our kids.

Scarcely two weeks passed before she grabbed my hand one afternoon to tell me she was pregnant with her third child. Quickly we were catapulted into conversations of morning sickness, exhaustion by lunch, and cravings. Sometimes she'd float names, curious about how they'd sound to an American ear.

One morning the phone rang, and I could hear the upheaval of tears. A routine visit to the doctor revealed that Tahany's growing son had a hole in his heart, making everything frightening. She could barely speak through the sobs; I don't know how she managed the road and the car. I instructed her to pull over in a nearby parking lot until she could slow her breathing. Then we met at her home to debrief together over sage tea.

Would her son survive this precarious pregnancy? Was this her fault? What could she do to keep him safe, buried deep in the folds of her womb? I had questions too—was this normal, were subsequent tests scheduled, when would we know more? "Call back the doctor's office and ask for a follow-up appointment," I instructed. "Can I do that?" she asked. "Will they allow me to come back so soon?"

It was then that I realized that for an immigrant with English as a second language, this situation was even more frightening. The country's medical apparatus was not second-nature, and Tahany was unsure what she was allowed to do on behalf of her son. "You can call and ask for another appointment, Tahany. Tell the nurse you have additional questions." So I wrote out a script for her on sticky notes and sat with her as she called the office. To her surprise, it worked! She could see the doctor in a few days for a follow-up visit.

Before the day arrived, we made a list of questions for the doctor, and we ended up driving together to the appointment. "Please make sure we get answers to all these questions—in case I forget or start to cry," Tahany said, putting the scribbled questions in my hand as we sat in the waiting room. Together we faced her fears. We asked questions. I asked the doctor to repeat answers more slowly so we didn't miss anything. Tahany and I held hands and heard answers that helped.

We would need to be careful, the doctor said, but he told us to try and not let fear take over. Easier said by him than done by the mother of a now-named boy in her belly.

Over the next months we weathered the high-risk pregnancy together as Tahany's husband, Khalid, worked long hours across town. I drove the kids to and from school, sat and sipped hot tea with Tahany in the afternoons, and drove us all to the park for weekend days when we needed shade and the kids needed space to run. Sometimes she whispered about her very bad luck. I countered with encouragement to pray: "Ask Allah to protect him, and I will implore Jesus to intervene." We did what mothers do, shouldering the risk together and working what small bits of rescue were in our control.

When Tahany's water broke and labor began in earnest in the evening hours, Khalid got her to the hospital. I rushed over. Having adopted my two children, I had never been in a birthing suite before, but Tahany wanted me to witness the birth of "our boy." I learned quickly about the necessity of a steady supply of ice chips. I supported Tahany's body weight in my arms as they gave her an epidural. While her husband tended to their sons, I watched over her like a mothering hen. When she pushed out her third son, we both exhaled. He was here—crying with life. And he was whole, with a healed heart. We lived through a miraculous rescue.

Tahany pulled me off the sidelines and into her pregnancy much like Jochebed did for Bithiah. She stood at a disadvantage as a Muslim, Palestinian immigrant. But the risk of birth forced her to reach out and trust me—or to take a chance that I might be different. And while the Spirit had already softened me toward my Islamic sisters, Tahany created an opportunity for me to enter her story and to disarm my own privilege for her sake. My eyes opened. I witnessed the struggle of immigrants and the ugliness directed at Muslim women. I learned how to be a friend and a bulwark against the discrimination. Lives were rescued—hers, mine, and his.

•   •   •

In the Exodus narrative, the Nile River cuts between the Hebrew and Egyptian communities, snaking through the land like a predator. Deep with meaning, the river is a character to be reckoned with. Ancients understood bodies of water to hold the power of life and death, and rumors abounded that monsters like Leviathan roamed the depths. A later Hebrew prophet named Pharaoh himself a monster who lurks about the Nile, assuming it belongs to him.[11] We do see those monstrous tendencies on display in the story at hand as he turns a life-giving river into a flow of tiny graves. Whatever the monster the Egyptians or Hebrews thought inhabited the Nile far beneath the crocodiles and hippos, the narrator wants us to see the waters as a metaphor of injustice.

What separates these two communities is a dangerous and deadly injustice. As we watch the women crisscross the currents, we ought not to mistake their movements for a simple swim; rather, they are confronting treacherous forces that seek to undo them and those they love. Jochebed braves the waters so that her son might survive. Jochebed's daughter, despite her young age, dives into the waters after her mother so that she can keep watch over her brother. And when Bithiah accepts the boy in her arms, the water of ritual cleansing is revealed to be the risk-laden river of rescue she must learn to navigate with the other women.

Watching these women enter into the waters of injustice to thwart pharaonic foes lights my imagination. What can I do to defy the pharaohs of my day and rescue those threatened by the destructive undercurrent of the rivers cutting through our communities? What are the leviathans of our own making—economic inequality, mass incarceration, inaccessible health care for the poor, gun violence—that beset us? What injustice plagues my zip code—and am I willing to follow the women into the rivers of risk and rescue? Will I hike up my skirt and wade in like Bithiah, joining the other women already buffeting the tide?

• • •

Investigating your own privilege does not come naturally. It requires some kind of in-breaking. For me, the first external threat to my ignorance about my privileged position in society was my husband, Claude. Born and raised in Burundi, and in extreme poverty, Claude saw my advantages clearly. When looking for a new job, I looked only at listings that interested me or that fit my self-perceived skill set. He told me about applying for any job available, any position he could possibly do, because when you grow up in a country with a 35 percent unemployment rate, you take whatever job you're offered. And when he moved to America to marry me, the challenge was not the unemployment rate so much as his black skin, his accent, and his initial status as an immigrant. He stretched his résumé to secure a job interview, he bluffed a bit in the interview, and he knew enough to mimic the emotions of the search team and to laugh at their jokes. He got the job—and served the organization well for years. But his job search process was different than the luxury I had to limit my survey to appropriate jobs that suited my preference. Even talk of paid vocation is a privilege, one it takes the average Burundian generations to earn. I slowly began to see how my light skin, my education, and my family's socioeconomic location shaped my sense of entitlement.

Over the many years of our bicultural marriage, I have had more opportunities to unmask the privilege that comes from my American citizenship as we travel internationally. My passport allows me to enter so many countries without even a visa or an interview. When I am in Israel-Palestine, I can go to Jerusalem or the seaside city of Jaffa, but as a Palestinian, Tahany cannot go to either place without special permission from the Israeli government. My citizenship affords me a freedom of movement and general sense of confidence as I move around the world. When I return home, the immigration officer stamps my passport, saying, "Welcome home." But for Claude, now a naturalized citizen, he often is required to submit to a secondary search. Membership really does have its privileges.

Living overseas drove the lessons home more deeply still. Even in a country populated and governed by Burundians, people often deferred to my light skin. I was given preference because I looked white, held an American passport, or was Western. Colonization set up a dynamic where my privileges operate in Burundi too. The little in US dollars I came with grew exponentially when converted into Burundian francs, another advantage that worked in my favor. If only I spoke French, as Burundi is a Francophone country, I would navigate the country like a queen. Nonetheless, I witnessed how my privilege traveled with me. It is a part of me that requires incessant inventory.

Recognizing my own layers of privilege, and this is by no means an exhaustive telling, took time. It happened over seasons of living in close proximity with someone who didn't have the same access and benefits that I did. Claude did manage to escape poverty and to graduate from university in France. He speaks multiple languages. He knows how to connect across cultural barriers and can figure out a fix in most foreign places. He is a force—and has cultivated his own kind of privilege in a world that handed me mine. In our conversations and experiences, Claude has never made me feel guilty for my privilege. But he has given me the opportunity to discover it and then decide how to respond.

What Claude and Tahany have done is help me develop my social imagination. According to Christena Cleveland, another privilege provocateur in my life, social imagination is "our understanding of how social structures (norms, beliefs, institutions) propel or impede an individual's movement in society."[12] When we are aware of our standing in society and what power we have relative to others, we possess a social imagination. The lingering impact of colonization in Burundi allows me, as a light-skinned Western woman, to have a certain measure of power that Burundian women don't have in their own country. My education gives me power that other women in America don't enjoy, not because they aren't intelligent but because they did not have the support (financial and otherwise) to attend college or seminary. But that power ceded to me gives me a platform to share my perspectives, while theirs too often go unheeded.

Where can we begin to investigate our own privilege? Cleveland recommends we start by taking a personal inventory of where we have power relative to others. What is your social position in your neighborhood relative to your neighbors—especially those who earn less or lack documentation? What power do you hold in your workplace compared to other workers? Or those who are unemployed? I used to joke that I was the most qualified volunteer in the church, as a woman with a master of divinity degree and my own biblical library at home. But the truth is that in church, my theological education *did* give me a measure of power. Do you lead the PTA, coordinate the staff at the local food bank, or run a ministry department for your congregation? Do people listen when you speak or give you deference for one reason or another? These are indicators of power afforded you by some measure of privilege. Taking a personal inventory of your privilege is the first step to cultivating a social imagination.

Once you can articulate where your power resides as a person with unearned privilege, the challenge becomes what to do with that power. We often talk about how Jesus emptied himself of his divine power when he was born a child, succumbing to life in a human body. The incarnation is a stunning picture of the relinquishment of power in order to more deeply identify with others—God removing the barriers between divinity and humanity. But Jesus not only let go of power; he also handled what power he did have on earth differently. Again, Christena Cleveland is instructive for us. She points out that Jesus also had a social imagination; he knew where he stood in society. He lived under Roman occupation in the backwater town of Nazareth, yes. But he did hold some amount of privilege as a man, as a Jew, as a teacher. And Jesus used his power not to enrich himself but to empower others around him. Cleveland highlights how Jesus empowered the woman caught in adultery who had no other defenders. He empowered the hemorrhaging woman by amplifying her voice among those to whom she was previously invisible. That is how to take our privilege and put it to work: not to just let go of power but to put it in service to others whom society refuses to see or hear.

This is the risk of the privileged, because empowering others often comes at a cost. After all, Jesus was berated incessantly for the company he kept, his reputation always at risk as he empowered women, those with disease, and other marginalized groups. But this is a lesson from the incarnation—to take inventory of our social standing, identify with others, and then empower them to more fully function in the community.

Most effective strategies for liberation will be initiated by those with less power, who possess hard-earned wisdom about what is necessary to move forward. Our work is to partner with those who can lead the way. This is what Bithiah learned from Jochebed's entrapment in the reeds and from the young Hebrew girl's clever questions. They needed her to submit to their ideas about how to save the boy. They needed her to use her privilege to empower their salvation strategies. And when she recognized what she could do in that moment on the shore of the Nile River, she allowed her social imagination to serve a liberation purpose, in partnership with the Hebrew women.

Engaging our social imagination is not something we do once and for all. Evaluating our privilege is a constant activity, much like a person in recovery who daily remembers that they must work in steps toward health and wholeness. We take stock, we strategize, and we partner with our neighbors for a more just world. I am grateful for those who have invited me into a better understanding of my place in the world: Claude and Tahany, but also Christena Cleveland, Lisa Sharon Harper, Melaney G. Lyall, René August, and the women of Exodus. They continually invite me to rethink my position and to realign my strategies in congruence with them, and for the sake of liberation.

◆   ◆   ◆

It's not only the waters we see, but also the daughters active along the shores. Pharaoh's decree ends with our beginning: ". . . but you shall let every daughter live."[13] Hebrew daughters will be allowed to live, and we will watch how it is that daughters, in general, go about living.

Levi's daughter, Jochebed, plays a key role in the story, but the tight focus is on Pharaoh's daughter, clothed in complicity along the edge of the Nile but disrobed, disarmed, as she interacts with women who are new to her. The Hebrew grammar points to her, Pharaoh's daughter, five times in succession.[14] The royal daughter is not exempt from the rescue operation set in motion across the river. She's lured into liberation by other daughters—a surprise to all of us.

Amram and Jochebed's daughter joins in too. She is not yet a mother but is every bit a daughter and so capable of full participation in liberation. There is something in the DNA of daughters, a fierceness not easily squelched. The men may be named, but the daughters move the liberation arc forward in the shadows of patriarchy. The scenes comprise a "series of small emergency maneuvers," as Brueggemann calls them,[15] which work against the imperial grain. Daughters, Pharaoh's or otherwise, are not easily daunted.

•   •   •

These daughters demonstrate the power to defy death from any side of the river. They show that the resistance is not limited to one tribe or one segment of the wider sisterhood but is open to any woman willing to enter the fray and work for freedom.

Pharaoh's own daughter might be seen as the height of privilege and incapable of feeling any urge for resistance. Indeed, it is often the case that such women are like Sarah and don't see the plight of fellow women. But Bithiah surprises us. The Spirit is at work in her, and Jochebed creates an opportunity for her to shake off her paralysis and to act on behalf of life. It's what Tahany did for me. It is what happens when we allow ourselves to be surprised by one another and accept the invitation, even the necessity, of relationship to navigate the waters of injustice. My friend Danielle is close to a young Muslim woman who resides in a nearby neighborhood. Over the years they have included each other in the thick and thin of their lives and have learned together how to help set each other free. My other friend Jessica and her friends, Burmese refugee families resettled in Austin, also live with openness toward one another and create ways forward that benefit their daughters. We are all daughters, all called to rescue the vulnerable ones regardless of which side of injustice we live on.

Rescue work is a series of small moves in quick succession, each person doing what she can to move vulnerable ones toward safety. The plan might not be clear at the onset, but every move matters. So we watch and respond like the youngest daughter in Exodus, whom we will meet in the next chapter. Hopefully, like her, we are poised at the starting line, listening for the starter gun. This is how we wait for the Lord[16]—or the next woman.

Chapter 5

MIRIAM

Freedom through Youthful Zeal

Miriam, crouched on the river's edge, watched her mother, Jochebed, maneuver toward the far side of the river. She followed her, curious what her plan was for her baby brother. She watched her mother place him in the reeds. Young Miriam stretched her imagination and tried to understand why she left him at Pharaoh's doorstep. Then she saw Pharaoh's daughter enter the water near the reeds. Once the baby was in the woman's arms, Miriam had to act fast.

Her question to the royal daughter—"Do you need a wet nurse?"—completed her mother's entrapment. One brave approach, one clever question, and the woman turned collaborator with her agreement. Now there was a way forward to save her baby brother, narrow though it be.

The young Hebrew girl hurried home to her mother. "Your plot worked!" she reported. The Egyptian woman was in, and needed a wet nurse. Jochebed was surprised, but eager to hold her son again. So the rescue operation continued as the two made their way back toward the woman waiting in the reeds.

Jochebed marveled at how Miriam cut the current with such determined strokes as she followed her across the river.

Her thoughts shifted quick like the tide: Was this a trap? Was Pharaoh's daughter holding the boy as bait? Could she be trusted? "This woman might be our lifeline—or our undoing," Jochebed said under her breath as she walked behind Miriam to the other side of the thicket. When Jochebed heard her son's hungry cries, however, she rushed to him without hesitation.

The Egyptian woman held her son. The sight of it knocked the wind out of Jochebed. Yes, it was the plan for her to save him. But up close, it stung. The face of the empire cradled her *matoki*. She reached for him and fumbled as she tried to get him to latch on to her breast with the Egyptian looking on. "Eat, *matoki*, eat," she whispered, turning her back to the woman. Hot tears raced down her cheeks. This was harder than she had anticipated.

Miriam stepped in. "I brought you a wet nurse."

"Yes. I owe you," Bithiah said to Jochebed, her own voice breaking. She sent her handmaid to fetch the money.

"You don't need to pay me to feed my son," Jochebed said, not taking her eyes off *matoki* as he ate. How could she take this woman's money, dirty Egyptian coins with Pharaoh's face on them?

"Consider it some small compensation for the troubles," Bithiah insisted. She composed herself and tried again: "Certainly there are hardships across the river."

"I do have another brother, and my father works long days firing bricks in the kilns," Miriam interjected. Then turning to her mother, she said, "We could use the help. And she can afford it."

Jochebed stopped listening. She moved further from the woman as she shifted *matoki* to her other breast. She hummed a song that was familiar to the Egyptian, one she had heard the

Hebrew women sing before. An oppressive sadness yoked them together, even amid the salvation operation.

Bithiah couldn't hide her tears. "My father does this—separating mothers from their sons and worse," she said. It came as a confession, an admission of her complicity. "But I want to help. I don't want more dead babies."

What could they say? In a world where no one was safe from Pharaoh's tyrannical whims, their only hope was to follow Miriam's lead and work together. Miriam still believed that her brother might save them all someday, so she helped the Hebrew and the Egyptian talk to each other. The only way forward, as far as she could see it, was an unorthodox collaboration no one had considered before.

•   •   •

One Jewish tradition tells of how Miriam spoke a salvific prophecy regarding Moses as he grew in his mother's womb.[1] As the rabbis read the enigmatic first verse of Exodus 2, "Now a man from the house of Levi went and married a Levite woman," it prompted a question. Amram and Jochebed already had two children—Miriam and Aaron—so why the mention of marriage this late in their family life? Was it for rhetorical effect only?

Rabbis are some of the most imaginative theologians, always pursuing the stories behind the story. Here they imagine the early days of the edict. Miriam was a child at the time. When news traveled across the Nile that Hebrew boys were doomed to drowning, Amram countered with an edict of his own. He decided he would not give Pharaoh any more sons to bury. Even though Jochebed was three months pregnant, her devout husband separated from her (sexually) and even divorced her. As the leader of the Jewish community, he encouraged the other men to do likewise. These men were going to fight fire with fire, as it were. In the world of edicts, they could see no other way.

But Miriam had young, clear eyes. If the imperative for Eden's children was to be always fruitful, always multiplying, then divorce thwarted God's original intent. She discerned that if there were no married couples and no babies, there would be no boys to bury, but also no girls to live. Her father's edict was harsher than Pharaoh's. And she told him so.

She also told him that her mother carried a son and he would bring liberation to their people. The specifics were unspoken, but the promise was deliverance.[2] So Amram married Jochebed (again), and she birthed a boy, as prophesied. Ecstatic, Amram kissed Miriam's forehead as a blessing. But months later, when he learned the boy was relinquished to the river, he soured. "Where is your prophecy now?" he questioned with the kind of anger that rises from the ashes of dashed hope.

The rabbis, filling in another perceived gap in the narrative, say this is why Miriam followed her mother across the river that dark morning—she was watching her brother. She waited for a resurrection of the words spoken to her. Maybe she wrestled with her own doubts, like we sometimes do, as she sat, riverside. Even at her young age, she had seen enough to know that blessings are complicated. Did the God who allowed slavery fail her again, this time allowing her own brother to perish before her eyes?

When Miriam saw the Egyptian woman reach for her brother, she did not wait for God. She waded in and hurried to her side to offer a solution to the boy's hunger pangs. Her prophetic listening had to be met by prophetic action.

•   •   •

Perhaps this is what we witnessed in Emma González and the students of Marjory Stoneman Douglas High School in the wake of the mass shooting in Parkland, Florida. A former student entered the campus on a February afternoon and opened fire. Seventeen people—students and teachers—were killed and many others hospitalized. It was another mass shooting in a country that has suffered too many.

The student survivors didn't waste time speaking out after the atrocity. Stepping up to the mic at a rally three days after the shooting, Emma declared that this would be the last mass shooting because they planned to organize for gun safety. She fearlessly called out the National Rifle Association and named the complicity of politicians who valued NRA donations over public safety. At seventeen years old, she led a call-and-response that galvanized youth across the nation.[3]

She and other students coordinated school walk-outs to protest gun violence in schools. They did interviews with news anchors and print journalists. They leveraged what they knew of social media to get the word out. They reached further still and organized the March For Our Lives, the largest student protest to descend on the streets of Washington, DC, since the Vietnam era. Not only that, but sister marches stretched across all fifty states and beyond our national borders. Emma and her friends became the icons of a new movement.

At the March For Our Lives, Emma stood as the anchor speaker. Before a crowd of 800,000, she remembered her friends who will never come to school anymore because a gunman took their lives. She stood in the spotlight, mostly in pained and powerful silence, for six minutes to coincide with the length of the actual shooting. Her tears testified to the truth of gun violence, her lament a social indictment.

Not everyone praised the Parkland survivors. Many legislators, pundits, and others looked down on their message, citing their youth as a knock against their credibility. How could high schoolers understand the complexity of the second amendment and gun laws? How could they be so articulate unless coached by adults with bigger agendas? Certainly they could not be trusted to shape the conversation around gun control, detractors said. But despite ridicule, dismissive words, and worse, the students spoke out, organized, and reframed the national conversation.

Maybe it is the gift of the young to see, without partisan lenses, the high contrast between right and wrong, safe and unsafe, life and death. Miriam knew that death edicts and divorce orders subvert life; Emma knew that more guns and lax laws mean more shootings that jeopardize public safety. The simple root system of what is right and good is often what feeds the young, free of political guile or vested interests in the status quo. Perhaps this is why the prophet Isaiah says a fresh shoot will need to grow out of the dead tree stump, a child leading the nation forward into a peaceable kingdom.[4] Only a child can imagine that nonviolence is possible and make a way where we see none. We hear Jesus extol the virtue of children, saying they exemplify God's kingdom and ought to be our role models.[5] But sadly, we all too often look down on the young, decrying their youthfulness instead of recognizing their witness and wisdom.

Emma and the others waded into dangerous waters, confronting the leviathan of the NRA and the national apathy toward gun violence and gun culture. They refused to let their age stifle their hunger for change. Emma spoke in the way I imagine Miriam spoke that day at the river's edge, cheeks wet with tears but voice strong with conviction.

•   •   •

"You braved a boy . . . ," Bithiah began, unable to finish the sentence.

"Yes," Jochebed said, gripping Miriam's hand, "*we* braved a boy in the shadow of your father's brickyard."

It really is hard to imagine how the first conversations unfolded between these women. The narrative is economical, speaking only of contract negotiations and quick successive commands to *Go! Nurse!*[6] But my own feminine intuition tells me there was more to their meeting than mere logistics.

After Miriam's coaxing, Jochebed finally drew closer, and stories must have been shared. How did you get the idea to make this raft? (The answer: my husband uses some of these same materials to make mortar for bricks, so I followed his example and innovated from there.) What have other mothers tried to save their sons? (Everything you can imagine—and some things you wouldn't ever dream of, born of utter desperation.) Does your other son work in the brickyards—he seems too young for such labor? (Yes—and yes.) I hear songs sometimes—usually at night—can you tell me what they say? (Miriam answered, describing the songs and translating the chorus.) I suppose it was a long while and many conversations before Bithiah could say what she most needed to say: Can you ever forgive me?

By then her Egyptian tears would not have been the empty tears of a privileged woman who intended no solutions. She paid regular compensation, far more than what was required, to help take the edge off some of the daily hardships. She listened to Jochebed tell of life growing up in Goshen—the loss of her father and several uncles, the maiming of a cousin. Each time they met, the crack in Bithiah's heart traveled deeper, but she kept asking questions and kept listening. It was a kind of repentance, her tears always a kind of cleansing.

These times spent together prepared her to adopt the boy. She learned bits about his culture and a rudimentary Hebrew vocabulary that she practiced mostly with Miriam, who was fairly forgiving. At first she included only her most trusted handmaids in these clandestine meetings by the reeds. But gradually she welcomed Jochebed and Miriam into her space within the gardens. Slowly she invited more of her friends with similar sympathies into the quiet conversations. But she still had to be selective, as many more women stood by the pharaoh and his policies.

A couple of times she even ventured across the river to meet with Jochebed in her neighborhood. Accepting Jochebed's hospitality was a sweet goodness that took Bithiah by surprise— what is it about sitting in someone's home? Shiphrah and Puah stopped by, curious about Pharaoh's daughter. Truth be told, these women who were the first to defy her father intrigued Bithiah equally as much. She was wise enough to know that she had much to learn from them about resistance. Their stories, holy and harrowing, pushed her to think deeper still about imperial policy. After these visits, she found herself more determined to subvert it at every chance she got.

Bithiah noticed that only in the privacy of her own courtyard, surrounded by her own kinfolk, did Jochebed get angry. The women would tell of a recent altercation, and their commiseration would give way to an outburst of anguish. Hot words flew faster than Bithiah could translate, and she watched Jochebed's face turn red as blood. This is where Bithiah discovered that suffering isn't only sadness, but also kiln-hot rage. In the safety of her own home, Jochebed was free enough to rail at the injustice of it all.

It wasn't easy for Bithiah to bear witness to the anger of the Hebrew women in the beginning. It felt as though the fits of fury were directed at her, given her connection to the regime. Her skin would bristle. Everything in her would want to cry out: *Not all of us are like him!* But she bridled her tongue, sat quietly, and absorbed the anger. She let it enter her, educate her sensibilities, and instruct her future actions. She became a frequent audience to their anger and eventually a participant in the outrage that welled up in her sisters.

Bithiah wished more Egyptian women would listen and help supplant the royal policies that killed boys and men alike. But so many women didn't care as long as Pharaoh covered their needs. Sometimes, when royal obligation required it, Bithiah would sit among the courtiers. She'd seethe at their ignorance and callous disregard for the Hebrew babies and mothers. These same women who raised her with kindness showed none for the women across the river. Was it only her royalty they honored, not her humanity? She found herself trusting the anger of the Hebrew mothers more than the kindness of her Egyptian aunties.

The women determined to hide nothing from one another. Jochebed and the midwives would express anger, Bithiah and her handmaids would weep, and then together they would exhale. The solidarity birthed between them created a strong network that traversed the Nile with regularity under the edict. The resistance movement grew in ways no one expected, crossing ethnic lines and pairing the privileged and oppressed in a sustained effort to save the most vulnerable ones.[7]

•   •   •

Of course none of this would have been likely without Miriam's bravery. She may have been a girl of no consequence from the wrong side of the river, but she dared to approach the royal daughter. Desperate times required her to push past fear and do the bold, pragmatic thing necessary to save her brother. Maybe this is a trait of her youth: inserting herself without calculating all that could be lost—or rather, because she knew who could be lost. The calculus of the young is different than that of adults; it's quicker and more clear-cut.

How hard was it for Bithiah to answer a girl half her age in a critical moment, holding a contraband baby? Or Jochebed— could she trust her daughter that it would be safe to brave another river crossing, that this was an opportunity and not a trap? Following a child is not intuitive or easy. But both women grasped for any alternative to Pharaoh's edict, and Miriam offered a fresh option for each of them.

Again I return to Isaiah's prophetic poetry. Sometimes our strategies to deal with the status quo are dead as a stump, and we find ourselves stymied. How do we remake a society that is prone to violence, where the wealthy routinely exploit the poor and those living on the margins are fodder for injustice? This was the prophet's context—and maybe ours too. We've given up on newness as a viable option. Instead we opt for the more reasonable tweaking of known mechanisms. We don't expect women and children to be of much help when it comes to establishing a new order. But as the adage goes, the thinking that got us into these predicaments won't get us out of them. Peace won't come in predictable ways.

A new shoot emerges, tender and green. It's as unexpected as resurrection—life out of death. We anticipate a lion but get a lamb. It's the young Miriam who emerges from the reeds to offer the next step for the women; it's Jesse's youngest son out shepherding who attracts God's attention (and anointing); it's the preteen Jesus sitting among the scholars of Jerusalem, both schooling and astonishing them. The Spirit surprises, empowering even the adolescent among us. It will be this very Spirit who will blow back the waters of the sea to reveal dry land, creating an exit where no one imagined one.[8] But we are getting ahead of the story . . . For now we'll fix our sight on the Spirit at work among the women and children.

．　　　．　　　．

Ahed Tamimi's childhood is rooted in the land of Palestine. She grew up (can you say a teenager is grown up yet?) in the village of Nabi Salih. Her family has been an active part of the struggle to protect Palestinian land. Her family home has been under a demolition order since 2010, and her community had been protesting weekly for years. The protests stopped only when Israeli soldiers injured over 350 villagers in a 2016 reaction to the village protests. Their home still stands but is constantly under threat.

Ahed has come of age under the incessant pressure and injustice of occupation. Much like young Miriam, she's watched the resistance. She's witnessed the indignity of the checkpoints and skunk water.[9] She's seen Israeli settlers ring her village and close in on her family's compound. She's endured frequent military raids of her home. She has lived through her parents' absences due to incarceration and has looked on as family members suffered harassment. Injustice and struggle shape the landscape of her life.

She's learned a kind of strength necessary for survival. When she was only eleven years old, she stood between an armed Israeli soldier and her mother as soldiers tried to arrest her and take her away from Ahed. On a separate occasion, she breached a safe distance, standing close with a raised fist, as Israeli soldiers circled her older brother to arrest him. Throughout her young life, she continues to speak out, demanding justice and relief, protesting alongside her community when necessary and defending her family members. She's been formed by occupation and the will to survive. She stands, like her family home, against the odds of a state set against her.

In December 2017, Israeli soldiers returned to Ahed's home once again. The Israeli soldiers had recently shot her cousin in the face, putting him in a coma and permanently maiming him. So when she saw the IDF uniforms approaching, she went out and met them. She got close enough to slap one soldier. Imagine that kind of bravery—but also that kind of anger. Her bare hand against a man armed to the teeth, her own intifada.[10] It wasn't much in the moment. But when the video taken by her mother went viral in the coming days, she drew the attention of the world and the ire of the IDF.

The soldiers came back to her home in response to the video. This time the soldiers came to arrest her for the slap seen round the world (or so it seemed). At sixteen years old, she was taken into custody and held—for months. Her mother, Nariman, was also arrested and held for her role in the incident.

Israel is known for harsh interrogation tactics, especially with Palestinians. Children are not exempt. The key aim is to terrify prisoners into speaking, getting them to confess so that they can be charged in court. But Ahed was a pillar of resistance in prison, keeping her silence, giving her interrogators nothing to use against her. As public pressure outside the prison mounted, her name and wild blond mane became a fresh icon of resistance.[11]

The hope was that jailing Ahed would squelch her impact and deter other youth from protesting the occupation. But Israel made an example of her instead, highlighting her capacity to resist and shining a light on the righteousness of her cause. She, in both her speaking out on the streets and her silence while imprisoned, inspired children in her village and beyond. Growing in courage, they marched more as they clung to her witness. Imagine a teenager staring down a soldier and refusing to speak, not backing down or breaking down. Imagine word escaping the prison and making the news at home. What a brave young woman.[12] She, like Miriam, defies the pharaoh of her day in ways that astound us.

♦   ♦   ♦

When Isaiah speaks, he moves us into a holy dreamscape where wolf and lamb, leopard and kid, lion and calf lie down in peace. Predators behave as if defanged. Despite their animal instincts, young cows and bears rest together without fear, as if their very nature has been recalibrated. And the lion eats straw with his brother ox, no longer preying on him or hungering for meat. What a utopian dream! Who could imagine such fundamental transformation? Yet Isaiah gives us this vision of radical reorientation—and says that a child will lead the way.

I watch young women like Emma González and Ahed Tamimi, aware that they are part of the grand conversion the prophet dreamed. I see Malala Yousafzai, shot by the Taliban at fourteen years old for going to school and returning to her hometown of Mingora in Pakistan six years later, alive and ever the advocate for girls' education. I look at Naomi Wadler, all of eleven years old, organizing a walk-out at her elementary school to protest gun violence and, weeks later, standing on a national stage at the March For Our Lives to acknowledge African American girls who are too often the unseen victims of gun violence. The sister march in Phoenix, Arizona, was initiated and coordinated by Samantha Lekberg, a sixteen-year-old high school student. These must be among the children Isaiah envisioned leading us toward nonviolence, justice, and God's peaceable kingdom.

•   •   •

On that Saturday morning, I marched in Phoenix, following the lead of Emma, Naomi, and Samantha. I walked with others into the plaza between our government buildings. Soon it filled with sunlight and people from every direction carrying signs and tambourines. There were students in their school colors, teachers, parents, and grandparents, all gathered in high spirits. I enjoyed reading the clever signs, especially from the teachers—about guns not being necessary school supplies; wanting books, not bullets; and how the only thing they want to pack for school is lunch.

But the signs that caught my attention were the ones that centered on the kids: "Follow the kids!" "We're with the kids!" "My generation will fix this!" And then this one: "What if these kids are the answer to your thoughts and prayers? Are you listening?" I felt the prophet calling out to us: The kids are speaking; are you listening? The children are leading; are you following? That's why I was there: to follow the students.

Samantha took the stage. She introduced herself as a local high school student and initiator of the Phoenix march. She told us how she reached out to students in Florida as well as fellow students across the valley. Together they learned how to coordinate this march. She learned, among other things, how to pull permits for public assemblies, coordinate volunteers, lead a network of student leaders, and partner with local activists and agencies. Then one after another, student survivors of gun violence stood and shared their stories. Young Latina women, young black men, white girls, and even a few mothers spoke of loss, resilience, and necessary public policy changes. Across the lawn, the crowd cried, cheered, chanted along with the student leaders.

Then we marched. Students took to the streets first to lead the way. Others held bullhorns: "What does democracy look like?" "This is what democracy looks like!" we responded. But again, it occurred to me that this isn't just what democracy looks like; it's what prophecy looks like when the Spirit moves it from the pages of sacred text onto the streets where we live. Our children are an answer to our most prophetic prayers, and they are capable of leading us to new places of peaceableness. My role is to follow their lead.

•   •   •

Miriam leveraged her youthful zeal into liberation work. She did not stay hidden in the reeds but stepped into the story, offering fresh opportunities for Pharaoh's daughter and her own mother. Her bravery commands attention. Her quick, clever thinking became the bridge two women needed to find each other. These women crossed not only a river but also ethnic and socioeconomic boundaries in order to form the next chapter in resistance: the Nile network. Together they furthered the work of justice, enacting a subversive strength under the nose of Pharaoh.

In this part of the story, the women are unnamed—they're just some man's daughters. Patriarchy and imperial structures often see women only in relation to powerful men, be it Pharaoh or Amram or Levi. But these daughters organize and resist, creating a new future on a still distant horizon. Nameless doesn't necessarily mean powerless, as they discover while sharing their stories, forging bonds of solidarity, and finding their collective strength.

Listening to young women might be a good start to liberative practice in our churches and communities. Miriam's descendants abound: Emma González, Ahed Tamimi, Malala Yousafzai, and more in our own neighborhoods. Do we seek them out? Do we see that today's leaders might be in the church youth group or on the high school debate team or helping care for her younger siblings after school? Are we willing to listen to their ideas and partner with them—and one another—for the sake of justice?[13]

Chapter 6

MOTHERS ALL

Freedom through Mothering

About two years had passed since Jochebed took her son across the river and back again, nursing him on milk and liberation lullabies. Did the Nile network conspire to save more sons from the watery grave? Did the women continue to share stories and brave dangerous waters? How many daughters of Egypt entered into wet-nurse contracts as a way to offer some measure of compensation to their co-conspirators? We're left to wonder.

The narrator tells us that when the boy was weaned, his mother brought him back across the Nile River one last time, a final relinquishment of her beloved son. This time she let him go not in an act of desperate and audacious hope but into the trusted hands of her friend. Pharaoh's house seemed the least likely place to find hospitality for him, yet she knew Bithiah would shield him and leverage all the privileges possible for her *matoki*. Jochebed ran her fingers through his silken dark curls one last time before she put him in Bithiah's arms.

"I want to tell you his name," Bithiah said, reaching for Jochebed's hand. "Moses." Naming a child was a parental pre-rogative and also part of the ancient adoption formula. When Bithiah named the boy, he became her son according to Egyptian protocol.[1] He was no longer *matoki*, no longer Jochebed's son.

Moses means "son" in the Egyptian language. The name was commonly paired with the name of a man or god, but Bithiah resisted the tradition. She knew that Moses wasn't the son of any Egyptian man, and she refused to saddle him with the name of these men of violence who meant his kinfolk harm.[2] He was simply *son*. But Mosheh (Moses) sounded like Mashah to Bithiah's Egyptian ear[3]—the Hebrew word for "drawn out of the water." She gave him a name that testified to how he was drawn out of the water by the women from both sides of the river. Every time she said his name, she remembered those who mothered him.

Bithiah's knowledge of Hebrew was clumsy but well in-tentioned.[4] She tried to speak words of connection as Jochebed let the child go. The deep dissonance wasn't lost on either of them. Jochebed waded back into the water and looked over her shoulder. She watched her *matoki* sitting on Bithiah's hip as they walked up the stairs, disappearing into the towering palace. Jochebed was both heartened and heartbroken—how could it be otherwise?

•   •   •

Burundi practices delay naming for children. This is partly a cultural tradition. Once born, the baby is called *bebe* for months and sometimes even a couple of years while the father discerns the nature of the child, speaking hope for the child's future or prophetic sense for his or her trajectory. When the father is ready, the child is named. Another reality that shapes this practice of delayed naming is rooted in the precarious nature of poverty. The infant mortality rate in Burundi is high due to food insecurity and the resulting malnourishment, plus the lack of access to medical services for most families. Many children simply don't survive.[5] So why get your hopes up with a name for a child who won't see a fifth birthday?

Since Claude crawled at his mother's feet, he was nicknamed *igipusi*, which means "cat" in Kirundi. Burundians associate big eyes with cat eyes, and one thing Claude has had from birth are those lovely, deep brown eyes and long, curled lashes. It wouldn't be until he survived past his second year that his father discerned his nature and felt confident in naming a son who stood a chance of living into adulthood. He named him Nkurunziza, meaning "good news," and it has been a fitting name ever since. It would be the later influence of European missionaries that would convince his father to rename him Claude.[6] But both names came after the precarious years when survival wasn't assumed.

We will never know what the baby boy was called as he crawled at the feet of his Hebrew parents. Did Amram call him *tinoki*, his little baby boy, as he bounced him on his knee? Or did Jochebed pat his back, whispering to her sweet *matoki* as she soothed him?[7] By whatever name he was known during that fleeting season, it would have been laden with affection. As long as he toddled around the house, he would have been loved—and well beyond his weaning. My friend Sarah speaks of the final weaning of her youngest child, the last to share the intimacy of nursing with her.[8] So tender are those hours, skin on skin, the bonding as mother and child burrow into each other. She tells about the last weaning coming sooner than expected and the accompanying sadness of the premature ending. Imagine Jochebed—knowing the final feeding ushered in another relinquishment. Maybe only a mother can fully know the loss of Jochebed, the lamentation that replaced her lullabies.[9]

•   •   •

Bithiah had time to search for an appropriate name for her soon-to-be son. She could have followed Egyptian tradition and named him after some man of influence. She might have considered a god as his namesake—the god of the sun that shone on him that first morning in the reed thicket, or the god of the Nile that cradled him until she waded into the water to hear his cry. But she chose *son*, unsullied by any association with the violence of gods or men. She opted for a name that meant family to her and that sounded like a testimony to the boy's salvific story at the river's edge. She alone discerned her son's name, thwarting the conventions of fathers and venturing into an unorthodox motherhood that wouldn't be entirely shaped by men.

Embedded in Moses by virtue of his name was the presence of both his mothers that day, standing between the river and reeds. He would be who he would be because they were who they were—together. The double meaning of his name points to sonship and salvation; it also reveals his dual membership in both communities[10] and enduring connection to both mothers.

Names connect me to my children and their mothers. Neither of my children were named by their birth mothers. The circumstances of their arrivals were too precarious, and each was relinquished before mother or father could discern their nature or hope for their future. But the nannies at the orphanage did name each child upon arrival. So I met my children and learned their Kirundi names and what they meant. Each name offered a glimpse into what the nannies saw in these babes: he is a friend, she is awash in goodness.

The adoption process required me to name Justin and Emma before their homecoming. On Claude's advice, I chose names that could function in both Burundi and the United States, as easily pronounced in French as in English. Once they were stateside and the adoption was certified by the state of Arizona, Claude stepped into the Burundian tradition. He took time to discern the Kirundi names for his son and daughter—what he sees in them and hopes for them. Turns out that after about eight months, he knew our son was light and our daughter a gift that keeps on giving goodness. He told me that it was in naming them that he felt the fullness of his mantle as father. And so our children add another name to their story.

The names given to my children reveal their identity and function as a record of who has loved them thus far. They know that Burundian women came first, some birthing and others nurturing them. They know that I entered the story next from a faraway place. They know they've been pulled close and crowned with promise by their dad. My kids and I regularly rehearse their litany of names, a blessing handed down from one woman to another like a favorite recipe. My daughter, now a teenager, loves when I sing her the song with all her names strung together like pearls. She wears them proudly.

Their names remind me that other women cared for Justin and Emma first. I parent in fidelity with their birth mothers and nannies. I know I am part of a larger network of women invested in the future of these children. The Kirundi names of my son and daughter are like seeds embedded in the soil of my soul, which sprout a lasting solidarity with these women, even all these years later.

• • •

The narrator plays a part in the naming of Moses as well, making his own theological statement. In a single name, he signals that deliverance is on the horizon. Moses foreshadows his people. One day they, too, will be drawn out of Egypt. As soon as the child's name is spoken, we know the trajectory is one of liberation.

But I'm drawn to Bithiah. She muddled the Hebrew meaning of his name, but her intent is clear: his salvation came through the hands of the midwives and mothers. Their saving work prepared the way for his saving work decades later. For now the focus is on this child rescued by the mothers who no one thought could dethrone Pharaoh. But it was only a matter of time before another pharaoh would know the name of Moses and witness God's deliverance of the Hebrews—mothers included.

• • •

The mothers' final meeting was months ago. Jochebed endured a final relinquishment of her *matoki*. Her loss was incessant. Her ache didn't end just because she knew Bithiah. She still must have cried a river of her own on the other side of the Nile that day and many days after.

Over all those months nursing him, she learned more about her *matoki*; now she knew the son she was letting go. She knew the sound of his giggle when she tickled under his chin or tugged his earlobes, how he crawled fast across the packed dirt floor when he heard Amram enter the house, how he came to a full stop when there was a beetle to study. She held many of his firsts, committing each one to memory for the long years of his absence ahead. The songs she sang to him lingered in her heart, though she retired the one about chariots being thrown into the sea because it hurt too much to sing his favorite lullaby without him there to smile and dance along. It didn't feel like much of a deliverance to Jochebed once she crossed back to the brickyards empty-handed.

Mother Jochebed suffered all these things. Logic reminded her that this was the best outcome she could hope for, her son safe with Bithiah and a long life ahead of him. But she knew the injustice of Pharaoh robbed them both of what was best: *matoki* growing under her roof and named according to her tradition. Still, she appreciated Bithiah's kindness to her family. She admired her for risking so much to raise *matoki* and for continuing financial assistance long after that last day at the river's edge. Pharaoh's daughter was now his mother, which was the bittersweet truth of it all.

For Bithiah, everything became real to her on that day. Now she held her son. She knew relaying his full identity to him was her responsibility now. Continuing his connection to his Hebrew heritage would be her yoke to carry. Also on her shoulders was the subversive work of educating her son to see injustice from the inside and imagine something different. She would raise him in Pharaoh's house but not indoctrinate him with the imperial values that produced endless quotas, death edicts, and dead boys washed up on the river's shore. She channeled the cleverness of Shiphrah and Puah and the bravery of Miriam all while preserving the memory of Jochebed. Mothers, adoptive or otherwise, are consummate multitaskers, meaning makers, and memory keepers.

•   •   •

When I brought my son home from Burundi, he was fourteen months old and the most beautiful brown boy with soft black curls atop his head and a banana-shaped dimple embedded in each cheek. Our church threw a shower to welcome him and his sister, Emma, into the family. The potluck fare covered the kitchen counter, balloons festooned the porch, and gifts piled high on a table in the living room. Our adoption was the occasion for a grand celebration!

About seven years later, I was watching the evening news on a February night. The news anchor reported a murder in Florida: a black boy killed in his suburban neighborhood, armed with iced tea and Skittles. When the picture of Trayvon Martin flashed on the screen, I froze. My son, now eight years old, bore a strong resemblance to the boy on the screen wearing a white hoodie.

I listened to how the reporter described Trayvon. I paid attention to how pundits, people at the coffeehouse, and even my own family talked about him. First came the assumption of guilt, not innocence. Then came the tropes of "thug" and the suspicion that he was a thief terrorizing the suburban neighborhood. Next were the questions about whether he, all of seventeen years old, was a good kid or a hardened troublemaker. I realized that this wasn't the same set of questions brought to bear when the teen in question had lighter skin. These were the questions posed about a black boy, and one who was the victim of gun violence—he was not even the one with the gun who pulled the trigger. A black boy was killed, and I watched how the world around me crucified him.

Night after night I watched the news coverage and studied the reactions to Trayvon and his family. *This is how they would treat my son if he were shot by the neighborhood watch group in my suburban community*, I thought over and over again. They would wonder if he lived around here, if he had a weapon in his pockets, if he was a thief. If confronted, and he became hurt or worse, they would question his character and not that of the shooter. My boy would not be allowed to be immature, scared, or innocent. I was shaken.

I overheard many good Christians talking about Trayvon Martin over their coffee and newspapers. The same kind of good people who so graciously welcomed my son with a balloon-filled party spoke about Trayvon as a monster who probably had it coming for one reason or another. I realized then that people did not see my son as a sweet, silly, energetic boy—they saw him as a black teen, with all the negative freight that comes with it. He was no longer an African orphan but a black man. I felt very alone and very scared.

This incident in Florida that shook me in my Arizona living room woke me up to the painful reality of how people see my black son, and how they see other black sons, and how they've treated black men for generations. I searched my own soul, because growing up in white spaces, I knew I was not immune; I had to repent of my own complicity in the kind of whiteness that would endanger black men and women. The creation goodness I saw in my own son I determined to see in the children of all the other mothers who worry about their black boys (and girls) on American streets.

Motherhood cracked me open. I saw not only my child but also the children of other mothers who love their sons as deeply as I love mine. I'd see the mothers and aunties shopping with their kids in Target, watch brown families sip sodas and split French fries in the next booth over at McDonald's, and see a black boy walking alone to school with a backpack slung over his shoulder—and I would know there was a connection between us. Because I have lighter skin, they may not have recognized the kinship we shared, and I understood that. But I walked with a new awareness that I owed those mothers my solidarity. I needed to be for them now and with them if things went sideways and they or their children were in peril. Mothering opened me to peacemaking in a different way. It made me recognize the interconnection and need for solidarity in societies that are often harsh on those with darker skin, those who are foreign-born, or those who speak with accents.

Unlike most mothers of black children, I had a choice to make. Since my husband, like my children, is Burundian and runs a community development operation in Bujumbura, we could choose to make Africa our home. So when our children entered middle school, we transitioned them to Burundi full-time. I wanted Burundi to have a formative role in Justin's identity, for him to have another story to reach for as he grew to understand what it is to be black in this world. Chances are America would show him plenty of discrimination and how people expect him to be a shoplifter or a thug but not necessarily a doctor or a president. I wanted him to have other choices when it came to developing his self-esteem and understanding how he could contribute goodness to the world.

Justin is Burundi-born and American-raised, and he carries both passports as he moves between these countries. He's studied American geography and the history of Burundian presidents. He mimics the dance moves of Michael Jackson and knows all the words to the Burundian pop we listen to on the radio as we crisscross Bujumbura. He is both Burundian and American. And his adventure, as I always tell him, is to discern what it means for him to be Burundian American in this world. What opportunities will your dual identity afford you in a world that struggles with binary thinking? How can you be a bridge for people or help connect different ideas from your cultures in innovative ways? These are the conversations we have, now that he is wrestling with his identity.

I don't want Justin to be only American any more than Bithiah wanted Moses to be only Egyptian. We both know that roots matter. For our sons to be fully formed, they need to know what it is to be Burundian, to be Hebrew, and to engage in the wrestling that ensues. As mothers, we must work to give them full access to the layers of their identity so that they can discover who they are and how to live at peace in the world. I feel a kinship with Bithiah, not only in her position of privilege that needed to be disarmed but also in her determination to make sure Moses knew he was as Hebrew as he was Egyptian. She didn't erase his Hebrew heritage; she didn't ignore it. She marked him with a name that said "you are both" and set him out on that journey of discovery. It is what I aim to do with my own son. I doubt either of us do it perfectly, and Lord knows we need help from our sisters to deepen our understanding. I think that in my own way, I, like Bithiah, set foot on a journey as a novice peacemaker that continues as I learn to navigate two cultures, various animosities, and what it means to oppose discrimination for the sake of peace for my son.

•   •   •

While in Bethlehem to meet peacemakers, our group of women mingled and spoke of possibilities amid our various conflicts. Lynne found me in the hallway. She told me about the work of father-and-daughter team John Paul and Angela Jill Lederach, which she intuited would be of particular interest to me.[11] Back on the tour bus, she shared with me (and all those within ear-shot) a story from their book.

The war in Liberia was brutal and known worldwide for the use of child soldiers to carry out unspeakable atrocities across their land. Once the official peace was negotiated, soldiers came home. Many were children traumatized by war who needed to be integrated back into society—but how? So many had wit-nessed the murder of their parents and were strong-armed to perpetrate violence against their own communities. Some tell of being forced to set fire to their villages, burning everything they knew and all they loved. Years in the bush robbed them not only of their childhood but also their humanity. Slowly they made their way to the only home they knew. The children stopped short of entering the village. They gathered under the generous branches of the large kum tree. How could they enter after what they'd done?

A few women were the first to approach the youth, now hardened and shamed. They brought food to them now and again. Slowly the mothers began conversations with the boys. Over time they ate together under the canopy of the tree, sang songs, and even prayed together. After months of care, the women determined it was time to bring the boys home.

The women did what Liberian mothers traditionally do: cut their children's hair. They were aware that the rough, mat-ted hair of the boys frightened many of the villagers. So the mothers created a hair-cutting ritual in the shade of the kum tree. Each snip of the scissors evidenced care; each fallen clump of knotted hair spoke of forgiveness. "Beyond words, cutting these boys' hair was an act of reintegration and of love."[12] The mothers walked into the village with the boys, allowing them to return and rebuild their lives as part of their community.

I've thought about this story many times—how the mothers took something ordinary and created an inroad for the boys to come home. They innovated with scissors. They made a way where there was none before, as the Spirit does. I remembered Bithiah transforming the mechanism of adoption into a tool for justice, allowing her to save one baby boy.[13] How she used the standard wet-nurse contract to facilitate a small act of reparation between her and one family. I thought of the Israeli and Palestinian mothers who make jam to make peace. I began to see with my own eyes how women take everyday things and create new ways to restore life.

As seasoned practitioners of peacemaking, the Lederachs stumbled upon mothering as a metaphor for social healing after witnessing mothers in Liberia and Sierra Leone mediating restoration in communities ravaged by civil war. They recognized how mothers create space for connection, understand the importance of rituals to foster belonging, and know the place of play in rehumanization.[14] There is something about the nature of mothers that allows them to see the child in even a perpetrator, the humanity of every person even in situations of conflict.

They tell about a Muslim woman, Haja Kassim, who was the lone female member on an interreligious council in Sierra Leone. The UN, in partnership with this council, accompanied them into the bush in an attempt to coax the young rebels from the Revolutionary United Front into negotiations toward a peace agreement. When the faith leaders encountered the rebels, the situation was immediately tense. The men made no headway in their talk with the leader of the group. Guns remained drawn. Haja observed the rebels, noticing that she could be their mother. Something rose in her, and she addressed them, "My children . . ." As she spoke in her maternal way, the rebels softened. They gathered around her more as children, less as soldiers. One boy cried, remembering his own mother. Another gave her what money he had, a small act of repair for damage he'd done. Her connection with these boys offered a breakthrough and allowed the council to engage them in talk of negotiations.

The Lederachs point out that Haja's experience as mother and role as leader "gave rise to a natural frequency of its own."[15] The modality of mother is often invisible and overlooked in peacemaking, reconciliation, and, in my own experience, community development work. But the work of mothers is often pivotal when it comes to outcomes that benefit communities. The same is true in the Exodus narrative. It's easy and too frequent that we miss the mothers who innovated under duress, who recognized humanity and began the liberative work that would set people free.

•   •   •

Mary received a visitation—and a holy announcement that the Spirit would overshadow her and she would birth God's child into the world.[16] How utterly mysterious that moment must have been for the just-betrothed woman. The messenger also told her she was highly favored.[17] Affirming yet frightening words for her to digest on that morning in Nazareth, alone with this word. Who would understand? She could barely understand it herself as she sat in stunned silence.

She remembered something else the angel said: her cousin Elizabeth was with child too. Given Elizabeth's advanced age, Mary knew this must be another miracle like that of Mother Sarah, and she found herself wondering if Elizabeth also laughed at the news. Since the messenger meddled with both of them, she knew she had to go to her immediately. She packed her things and hurried south to a small village just a stone's throw from Jerusalem.

Luke's Gospel is unclear as to whether or not Elizabeth knew Mary's condition before her arrival. But when her cousin crossed the threshold into her home, her body surged with emotion and a bit of intuition. Her child leapt inside her. She was filled with the Spirit on the spot. She meant to say a simple hello but instead exclaimed, "Oh Mary, you are blessed among women!" It was a morning of rolling revelations as the mothers-to-be embraced and started to share their stories as best they could.

Imagine the women sitting side by side in a patch of sun, weeks into the visit. Elizabeth, looking at Mary, insists she is maturing before her eyes. "It's deeper than the pregnancy glow women talk about around the well, Mary. You remind me of Mother Eve. You are fruitful; you are multiplying. Isn't this what we are made for?" The young Madonna cradles her own belly, saying, "Overshadowed by the Spirit or not, we are contributing to the goodness of creation."

How good to be in the company of another mother who understood! Both women experienced visitations and heard holy words about their sons. Both felt a bit dumbfounded in the aftermath—one too old, one untouched, but both with child. Cloistered together for three months, they tried to untangle what was happening to them. They pondered what was to come for them and their sons. These would not be ordinary boys with ordinary lives. They would shake the status quo. They might draw attention to the family in uncomfortable ways. Is there any chance this will elevate our status in the community? No, they agreed. We will be misunderstood and misrepresented; it will be our maternal burden to carry. Still, they believed their boys would change the world as they knew it.

Based on the messenger's words, these boys would upend injustice and maybe even usher in God's deliverance. It would likely be a messy but nonetheless mighty work. How good it is to not be alone, to have each other as they gestated these boys and witnessed them become revolutionary men.

Elizabeth and Mary were mothers of the movement that would sweep through first-century Palestine. John the Baptist would stand in the Jordan River and make baptism available to everyone outside the temple complex, challenging the religious leaders of the day. He would raise the hackles of Herod and his wife for naming their immoral union. He would be jailed and beheaded for his prophetic witness. Jesus would befriend the poor and marginalized people of the empire, speak of jubilee economics that confront the imperial economy, and usher in another kind of kingdom. He would be a threat to the temple and empire alike, and crucified as a terrorist. Their mothers would not only gestate and birth revolutionaries but also lose them at the hands of the law-and-order men of their day. Yet Jesus would see his mother at the foot of his cross, her presence like a final embrace as the Jerusalem sky darkened. She was his co-conspirator from beginning to end, mothering him even unto death.

•   •   •

The room sat in rapt attention as Bryan Stevenson stood among us at the headquarters of the Equal Justice Initiative in Montgomery, Alabama. He began by sharing his first experience of racism. His family was at a hotel, and he wanted to jump in the pool with all the other kids. As soon as he did, the other kids were scooped out of the water by parents. The white families did not want their kids mixing with him and his siblings.

Next he told us of his grandmother. She would pull young Bryan close into her chest in a tight hug. "Do you feel my love?" she'd ask him. She would keep holding him and keep asking him the same question until he answered in the affirmative, that he could feel her love around him. She did this all the time, enveloping him in her love-laden embrace so that he knew what her love around him felt like, even when she was not there to hold him. As he grew older, and she passed on, this became a lasting gift she left her grandson. He could close his eyes and feel her love in moments when he felt scared or alone or left out. And as a black boy growing up in the South, he remembered her hugs often. She found a way with what she had—her two strong arms—to convey deep belonging and presence to Bryan. This is another instance of creative mothering, a way to keep a boy grounded amid experiences of discrimination and things she could never imagine this one-day civil rights lawyer would live through.

I have a black son of my own. A couple of summers ago I began hugging him longer, asking him if he could feel my love around him. At the end of the summer, when I traveled to the States for work, I told him he could remember what my love felt like even when we were apart or when he was afraid. Later when we reunited, he told me he always knew what my love felt like around him. Recent months have offered us fresh teenage challenges, and again he told me he knows what my love around him feels like during his dark times. He told me that my embrace helps him find the courage to make better choices. I owe that to the creative genius of Bryan's grandmother, who knew how to innovate a means for tangible presence of mother love for our black sons facing a harsh world.

•　　　•　　　•

Sister Teresa was a vowed member of the Sisters of Loreto, a teaching order of nuns in the Catholic Church. In 1946, she took a train to Calcutta for an annual retreat. During this season she responded to a deeper call that had been pressing upon her for some time: to serve the poor directly. It almost seems mysterious how she moved from sister to mother, but in her move toward the poor of Calcutta, she became Mother Teresa. The rest of her ministry was dedicated to caring for the sick and dying. A hallmark of her life was her capacity to recognize the humanity of the destitute, those the world did not see.

This extraordinary woman reminds us of a common truth: mothering is a verb. Mothering is not exclusive to women who give birth but, rather, a hallmark of women who sponsor life in the myriad ways they care for those around them with compassion, recognizing the humanity of young and old, privileged and oppressed, those in sickness and those in health. We are mothers when we generate life as much as when we advocate for the quality of life.

•　　　•　　　•

The Gospels tell us a bit about how two mothers gestated and birthed their sons, but what piques my curiosity is how they raised revolutionaries. They did not leave us a curriculum to follow or many bread crumbs, for that matter. All I have is my own imagination to suppose how they raised children strong enough to be in the empire but not of it.

I think back to Mother Jochebed, who must have sung liberation lullabies to her children under a luminous moon. Songs of creation and the God who spoke light and life into being with love, songs about Noah's family surviving floodwaters with the help of God (and a dove), songs about Abraham leaving Ur for the new land God promised to show him, and about Patriarch Joseph with his dreams, multicolored coat, and adventures in another kind of Egypt. Jochebed sang her lessons into her youngest son's spirit as she nursed him. They were the same songs she sang for Aaron and Miriam, trying to give them a vision beyond slavery and death.

I remember how Miriam watched her mother brave the Nile River with the makeshift raft carrying her baby brother. How that example of a clever and courageous mother fed her own sensibilities. If her mother could brave the waters and the Egyptians lying in wait, then so could she. If her mother could sing songs of Hebrew history, she could compose songs of Israelite futures. We cannot underestimate the power of parental example in the formation of our children's capacity for liberation dreams.

I've listened to one sermon by Walter Brueggemann over a hundred times since he preached it in 2008—which is slightly embarrassing to admit, but not an exaggeration.[18] In it he describes the work of the New City in the book of Isaiah, and how impossible it sounds to our modern ears. Then he mentions the thousands of young children he noticed in the Sunday school program at this megachurch. "They must belong to some of you," he laughs as an aside. Except it isn't an aside; it is the crescendo of this master sermon. "Imagine if your kids see you eating with people unlike you—and they grow up to create new immigration policy. What if they see you care for the sick, and they grow up to fix the health-care system?" Not once have I listened to this sermon without weeping at the thought that my actions have that potential in the life of my children.

What if our actions as parents are the catapult for our children to make possible what we only can dream about? Consider our actions: Are we planting those seeds that will become the holy harvest of the New City at the hands of our children or grandchildren? Certainly Miriam followed in her mother's footsteps. And Moses followed the liberation trajectory set by the mothers in his life—Jochebed and Bithiah but also all the other women who mothered him with liberative verve.

Mothers shape our worldview, our imaginations, and our sense of what is possible. They give us language for lament and capacity for liberation. They are the arms around us when we are unsure or unsteady and the voice we hear pushing us forward into a new land where we are all free. They nurture in us the potential to be revolutionaries in whatever Egypt we find ourselves in, against whatever pharaonic forces we must confront. When we mother, at our best we are entering the work of peacemaking as we see the humanity in every child, every person, and work toward a viable and vibrant life for all.

Chapter 7

THE SEVEN SISTERS OF MIDIAN

Freedom through Solidarity

R aised under a royal roof, Moses learned the ways of Egypt and wore them with ease. He was mature and well established in the empire. He possessed wisdom and knowledge, believed to be recompense for his virtuous mother, according to the Qur'an.[1] Jochebed's willingness to relinquish her infant son is remembered. And the Qur'an credits Moses's good character to his birth mother.

The narrator of Exodus says that once Moses had grown up, he went out to his people and saw their forced labor.[2] Bithiah did well—her son knew the Hebrews were his kin by birth. His desire to connect with the Hebrews and his curiosity about his origins were natural.[3] But what he witnessed angered him, the injustice so obvious.

Moses arrived at the brickyard and saw his people slaving under the taskmasters. He moved to the far edge of the work site, where an Egyptian was haranguing a worker. He watched the interaction escalate until finally the slave driver shoved the man to the ground. Moses looked around and, seeing no one else nearby, struck back on behalf of his Hebrew brother. The taskmaster was dead.[4] At the site of injustice, his instinct was to stand for his kin, even if they did not recognize him as one of them.

The next day Moses returned to the brickyard. From afar he heard yelling and saw jousting bodies. He hurried to help, only to find that the conflict was between two Hebrews. Instead of solidarity, he saw the tension trauma bred. As the men battered one another, Moses tried to advocate for a just outcome between these brothers. But they didn't welcome an Egyptian meddling in Hebrew matters and told him to mind his own business. His verdict was unwanted.

In that moment Moses woke to the harsh reality that he was an Egyptian in appearance. He looked like an outsider to them, and their disdain toward him was now apparent, as one spit in his direction. Because they had no reason to keep his murderous act secret, he was a marked man. This time even his Egyptian mother couldn't protect him from Pharaoh's wrath. If he sought solidarity in the brickyards, he found none.

In recalling this episode, we catch a fragrance of Moses's two mothers, Hebrew and Egyptian. I appreciate the qur'anic narrative's gentle nod to Jochebed, the recognition of her loss imprinted on her son. It allows me to imagine that her ability to let her *matoki* go into Bithiah's care created an avenue of blessing that would serve him well into his adulthood, contributing to his liberative trajectory before he even fully embodied it. I admire Bithiah and her more covert influence beneath the surface of the biblical text. As an adoptive mother, I know something of what it takes to preserve original identity and not forget that your child isn't only yours. Bithiah raised Moses with the awareness of his dual identity and gave him the freedom to pursue it. Her fidelity to Jochebed and the other women across the river endured. Moses fled with the aroma of his mothers clinging to his skin. He also carried the struggle of discovering his true identity between his two mothers and their cultures.

•   •   •

The desert of Midian was inhospitable terrain—hot, arid, and, some said, populated by descendants of Ishmael. Mother Hagar, who ran back and forth to find water for her son, haunted this land. She stumbled upon Zamzam and, according to the Qur'an, founded a nation. Every land has a mother, and the woman who saved her son against all odds presided over this thin space.

The Jewish people possess a rich tradition around wellside meetings. Isaac met Rebekah as the result of an interaction at a well, and Jacob met the love of his life, Rachel, at a well too.[5] Wells held the potential for romance.[6] Whenever there was mention of a patriarch and a well, the listener waited for the arrival of the wife-to-be. But wells in the ancient Near East were also functional spaces where shepherds and sojourners met.[7] Women trekked to and fro daily to draw water for household needs, and others found the well a place of respite from the scorching sun.

It is no wonder Moses ended up sitting by a well in Midian. He was beyond Pharaoh's reach but in foreign territory. He rested on land between cultures, between traditions, and it seemed to mirror his own internal wrestling between nature and nurture.

Maybe the activity around the rural well kept him happily distracted from dueling thoughts. Animals moved across the landscape as herdsmen came to draw water for their cattle and sheep. A long line of camels shuffled down from the horizon, the merchants sending water boys ahead to fill troughs for their eventual arrival. Moses observed more men around this well than most. Tending livestock was a man's job, so it made sense enough to him as he overheard their desert dialects negotiating the terrain.

He must have dozed off in the warmth of the morning sun. He awoke to the sounds of sheep bleating and women organizing. He counted seven women working the flock—a few guarding the edges of the mob while the others drew up the water and filled the troughs. The musculature of the women revealed that they did this work daily. They weren't the wispy waifs he imagined when he heard his first mother tell stories about Jacob and the winsome Rachel. But the spell of childhood stories broke when some surly shepherds pushed their way to the well's edge.

No sooner had the men pushed aside the shepherdesses and scrambled their flock than Moses jumped to their defense. He fended off the shepherds. Then he finished what the sisters had started and watered the sheep. The narrator is economic in his description, offering no fast-paced, show-of-strength action sequence. Moses simply defended the women, drew water, and tended the flock, the narrator says. He was a deliverer, not a hero.

The seven sisters arrived home early. Their father noticed—maybe wondering why they cut the workday short. "An Egyptian helped us at the well," they said in sistered unison.

"Go invite him for dinner," he responded. Hospitality was the best way to demonstrate gratitude and learn more about this man.

Some of the sisters stayed back to finish the last few chores before nightfall; others began preparing the meal for their guest.

Two walked back to the well to offer the invitation. "Imagine if we could get home hours early every day," the one mused.

"Maybe there'd be time to marry," the eldest teased.

"Do men respond only with respect to other men?" the younger asked as a more rhetorical question, since they both knew the answer in their male-dominated landscape.

"If we were sons and not daughters, things would be different. But we are all our father has," the eldest said, smoothing her hair as they approached the Egyptian.

Moses noticed her calloused hands as she pulled her hair back, revealing dark eyes and sun-bronzed cheeks. "Our father would like you to join us for dinner tonight," she announced, "to show appreciation for your kindness to us today at the well."

"You are sisters? All seven of you?" he asked.

"Yes, sisters and shepherdesses," she confirmed.

"I can see that," he said as he looked at her hand, hardened by work. As the three of them walked back to the father's tent, he asked more questions. "Those shepherds . . ."

"Every day," she sighed. "But we've learned to manage them in our own way."

Today the Egyptian provided relief, but tomorrow would be more of the same. That was the truth of things for a woman, even a strong and skilled one, in a man's world. Zipporah thought of this as she fell asleep wondering what would come of the Egyptian man in Midian.

◆　　　◆　　　◆

Moses stands in the spotlight of the narrative. He is a man with his own agency. In this unfamiliar territory, his true identity begins to surface. Once, his mothers drew him from the water in defiance of Pharaoh; now he's drawing water out of a well for the seven women to mete out some measure of justice against the men. The narrator shapes the story so that we will see Moses taking the next step into his destiny as a deliverer.

The daughters of Midian exist in the shadows of the story, the backdrop to Moses's movement toward deliverance. It's the way of patriarchy to see women in relation to men, to see seven shepherdesses as daughters of Reuel.[8] These seven women worked the flock, laboring long days because there were no sons to manage the herd. They *drew water* on a daily basis, and since the narrator uses this as a metaphor for deliverance, then we can say these women performed daily deliverances on behalf of their father's flock as competent laborers.

Cutting through the patriarchal perspective, I see the women in relation to one another. They are seven sisters, seven hard-working women. In a world of wild beasts, harassing shepherds, and limited resources, it wasn't easy to be a shepherdess. Survival required skill, strength, and solidarity. They learned how to work together, building on one another's strengths and tending to their own relationships in order to remain a cohesive unit in the harsh desert territory. Their solidarity borne of necessity, not shaped by oppression, sustained the family. They banded together to live well and to survive the worst in an unsure climate. You might recall that *seven* in Hebrew literature means something. The full complement of women, the complete sisterhood, navigates the desert and gets the work done. What if we saw these women first as hard workers? Think of their calloused hands, strong backs from repairing fences and pulling lambs out of birth canals, muscular arms due to daily drawing water from stingy wells. Imagine them as good shepherds, the gatekeepers for the sheep. Leading the herd to green pastures and filling troughs with water. Daily protecting the sheep from predators, fending off those that came to steal, kill, and destroy. The sheep would know the sound of their voices.[9]

Shepherds daily harassed the sisters. Still, the women had to draw water, or the flock would perish. This meant the sisters had to devise strategies for dealing with the men who regularly blocked their well access or otherwise hindered their efforts. Did they employ the fabled feminine wiles, or did they have other tactics that allowed them to secure water? Did they simply hang back and wait until the shepherds finished before they made their way to the well for their turn? Did the eldest negotiate with the men sometimes, perhaps outwitting them on her better days?

When Moses witnessed the haranguing, he intervened to save the sisters. It was his nature, as the narrator keeps pointing out at every turn in this passage. He preempted the shepherdesses' usual strategy to counter the aggressive men and secure the necessary water.

Isn't this too often the case: women spending more time doing the same job not because they are less capable but because men who make access difficult on a daily basis slow their work? For too many women, managing male dominance and even harassment in the workplace is part of our job description. Couldn't we all get home earlier if we simply enacted equity?

The seven sisters weren't romantic maidens roaming the hills with a few sheep, a mere foil for Moses's self-discovery. They were shepherdesses with strong hands and clever strategies for managing the terrain. The sheep knew their voice and followed them. Their father knew their work ethic. They trusted one another to run the herd and have each other's backs. Solidarity, not just biological sisterhood, was required to survive.

•   •   •

I met Idelette McVicker in Kenya at the 2010 Amahoro gathering[10] that Claude and I hosted. We clicked during our very first conversation as we spoke of justice, our connection to Africa, and our bicultural marriages. Idelette had recently launched *SheLoves Magazine*, an online publication that delivers good news about and for women with a commitment to Jesus, justice, and the global sisterhood. She needed partners who could help create thoughtful content. In those embryonic days of our friendship, she invited me to write what would become a monthly reflection in the magazine.

Sisterhood, a word that rolled off her tongue like a song in her South African lilt, was unfamiliar to me. She spoke of sisterhood like it was the Holy Grail, full of promise and mystery. She was on a quest to find this sisterhood, to expand its reach. Even though I wasn't one given to women's ministry or even women's Bible studies, I was intrigued. It was a dynamic I didn't quite understand. But I believed in her—so I stretched beyond my comfort zone and agreed to write for women. Once the Kenyan gathering ended, she returned to Canada with her family and new magazine while I returned to Burundi with my family and our development work.

My newfound sister and I were separated by miles but joined in purpose to educate, encourage, and connect women. For the first time, I wrote in public, beyond the pages of my journal. I also wrote with women in mind. I started to explore how I fit into a larger narrative of women, what shared purpose we might have beyond the genteel ministry of my mother's generation. I wrote about our liberation mothers: Mary and her Magnificat, Ruth the Moabite, and the women of Exodus (mostly

Miriam back then). I worked, month by month, at articulating a theological vocabulary for our growing tribe of women. We'd have conversations in the comments section of articles about shalom, jubilee economics, salvation oracles, and God's preferential option for the poor. I was finding my place among women who hungered for justice. They wanted to learn about the imperatives from Scripture, but also implement them in real time. And this is where Idelette shone like a beacon: she mobilized the women not only to love justice but also to act justly in their world. The community she shaped simultaneously formed me and my sense of what was possible for women of faith in league with one another.

About a year or so later, I wrote about a community of Batwa people in Bubanza, a province just outside the capital city of Burundi, for *SheLoves Magazine*. Claude and our development team began work with these 660 families to bring about a better kind of life for them. Our initial project was securing identity cards for all the adults, starting with the women. This surprised the community, since it pushed against the patriarchal norms of Burundian culture. But we saw these women in their own right as mothers, wage earners, and people worthy of citizenship.

Idelette reached out to me one afternoon. "How much does an identity card cost?" she asked. "The equivalent of $12," I answered back. "How many more women need cards?" I told her that 425 women were awaiting their cards. She did the math. Then she reached out to the *SheLoves* community of women and asked them to consider raising $5,100 to fund identity cards for the remaining women in Bubanza as our Valentine's Day love action.

I showed Idelette what a Burundian identity card looks like: a powder blue, trifold piece of cardstock with a square photo, a fingerprint, and an official stamp. Before long we were asking people to buy blue "roses"—that is, identity cards—instead of red roses for Valentine's Day! Husbands and boyfriends bought dozens for their beloveds, and women bought them for their friends. The sisterhood of *SheLoves Magazine* raised $7,212 in two weeks for 601 cards—enough to underwrite identity cards for all the women of our community, plus many of the men.

Solidarity took on flesh for me during those weeks. Our *SheLoves* sisters embodied their commitment to the women of Bubanza. They said no to red roses in favor of blue identity cards for their Batwa sisters. They decided that Batwa women possessing ID cards and becoming full citizens of their country mattered. They decided that love looked like identity for their sisters, not Hallmark cards and conversation hearts.

That summer Idelette and another SheLovely, Tina, traveled from Canada to Burundi to visit me—and the women of Bubanza. Our reunion in the tiny airport of Bujumbura was surreal; my sisters were here in the heart of Africa! They cleared their calendars (and customs) to be with me. My cup overflowed as we pulled bulky suitcases to the car on that humid summer day.

The next morning, we piled into the car with Claude and drove out to Bubanza, about forty-five minutes north of the capital city. We pulled into the community compound, where hundreds of Batwa women awaited our arrival. They sang and danced under a corrugated tin canopy to welcome us as our feet hit the ground. Claude had a surprise for us. He held in his hands the final batch of blue ID cards that had just arrived from the government office. He handed us the stack like a bouquet of blue roses. The three of us, along with René, who joined us from South Africa, would hand out the final two hundred identity cards on behalf of the *SheLoves* sisterhood.

The women gave us seats of honor in their circle, which we felt unready for and unworthy of. As each blue card passed through our hands, goodness increased between the women. Our space filled with long hugs, joyous laughter, shy grins, and clasped hands. And because this was Burundi, there were speeches. Donatilla, a community leader, stood erect, holding her new identity card above her head. "Now no one can harass me when I walk to the market. They can't hold me in a jail cell because I am undocumented anymore. Now I am a human," she announced. Another woman declared: "We are unstoppable now!" to the cheers of all the women gathered. It was a new day for these Batwa women—and something simultaneously dawned in me. Sisterhood birthed solidarity.

Idelette took her turn in the center of the circle. I don't remember what she said. I remember her bare feet on ground made holy by a sisterhood of women that was possible only in the imagination of God. I can still see the tears streaming down her ruddy Afrikaner cheeks. Her body told the story of a woman humbled in the presence of her sisters, a woman aware than she stood deeper in her identity that morning because they were more fully standing in theirs, identity cards in hand.[11] This is what the South African concept of *ubuntu* teaches us: that we are interconnected and fully human only in relationship to one another. In that circle of women, we were our most human, our most humble, and our most glorious. This was the day I experienced solidarity as the incarnation of sisterhood. I finally learned what Idelette knew: that sisterhood opens the door to reciprocal transformation whereby we all become more human and more free together.

It's not lost on me that my first taste of sistered solidarity held elements of the socioeconomic imbalance created by generations of colonization. Women with access to Western resources were helping those who lacked representation and resources in their own country, a land once usurped by European nations and still carrying the brokenness of colonization. Yet our coming together cracked us all open for transformation. Witnessing the new freedom of our Batwa sisters would recalibrate our eyes when we returned to Canada and America. We would seek solidarity with neighbors in our home nations.

Ever since that day, I've remembered how my own freedom is intertwined with the freedom of other women, at home and abroad. I close my eyes and see the Batwa women dancing, singing in unison, and waving their cards. They smiled and embraced. This, you could see, would change things for them. For years they walked kilometers together to get water for their families, sat with each other when unlawfully jailed, and shared in the struggle to survive the inhospitable terrain of extreme poverty. The true story was how they would carry on together, newly armed with these cards that formalize their identity, their rights. We helped with the IDs, but the women had been laboring together long before we arrived and would stay shoulder to shoulder long after we left in our big jeep. Their solidarity, with or without our blue roses, taught me about the sustainable strength of sisterhood.

·　　　·　　　·

As an adopted person, I've lived with the reality of a hidden history. My origin story remains unknown to me, sealed by a court order for almost fifty years now. I know little about my birth mother—just that she was Mexican and an accountant at the time of my birth. When I was three months old, my parents adopted me. Even though my adoptive mom is also of Mexican heritage, I was basically raised as a white evangelical.

Growing up, we always had tortillas and hot sauce in the house. A favorite family appetizer was guacamole and chips. This wasn't because we were Mexicans but because we were Californians. We also loved steamed artichokes, garlic bread, and all kinds of olives. I don't remember ever feeling Mexican; it wasn't an identity marker for me even though it was the only thing that connected me to my birth mother. I was a California girl more than anything.

During my forties, a series of small seemingly disconnected epiphanies confronted me with a strand of my almost forgotten identity. I returned to the Catholic Church and recognized her as my mother church. I discovered that I was a liberation theologian at heart. I felt a draw toward Latina women and was especially hungry for theologies articulated by Latinas.

I picked up *Mujerista Theology* by Ada María Isasi-Díaz. It was with great intention that I started reading a Latina liberation theologian. Her story drew me in and her thinking challenged me. But her final chapter revealed an unexpected fullness. She spoke of the way Latinas practice their faith—lighting candles to keep vigil, creating space for Mother Mary in their home, and holding a rosary as they pray. She was describing me.

◆　　◆　　◆

When Claude and I moved into our first home, I bought a statue of Mary. I didn't go looking for the Madonna. Instead the sable-colored mother caught my attention among all the other Mexican artwork at a roadside stand along the Arizona highway. She became the first guest in our home. I set up an iconostasis where I hung my collection of icons: the Holy Trinity, Jesus rising from the tomb, John the Baptist, Peter and Paul embracing in reconciliation. I lined up blue-glass votives in my office and lit them when I prayed and when I wrote. I bought a rosary (not having owned one since my auntie gave me one as gift for my First Holy Communion) so I could pray it before midweek mass. I thought this was merely my way of embodying my faith, slowly developed over years of following Jesus.

But when I read about the substance of Latina practice, I found myself in the company of my Hispanic sisters. My eclectic collection of faith practices was not unique to me but pointed to my connection to a community I'd forgotten (or never knew). "I'm more Latina than I thought," I wrote in the margin of *Mujerista Theology* after reading the final page.[12]

A couple of years later, I traveled to New Mexico to gather with a small group of friends. The group was diverse—so many people of color and, I noticed, several Latina sisters. I savored our conversations about contemplative practice and justice, especially as we annotated the ideas with gleanings from our own histories and cultures. I felt such deep resonance with Alexia Salvatierra, Lisa Sharon Harper, and Alexie Torres as they spoke with theological insight and sharp discernment.

There came a time in the weekend, as is often the case in mixed groups, when we needed to untangle some dynamics related to race. The decision was made by a diverse team of leaders to break up for some conversation, and then reconvene to debrief together. "White folks downstairs, everyone else stay upstairs." As everyone began to relocate for the next session, I froze. For about thirty seconds I did not know where to go, which group I belonged to. I am Mexican by nature but white by nurture. If I stayed, would the women of color give me side-eye?

Would they question my presence there or send me downstairs? I decided not to risk offending them and went downstairs with the white people. And since I was, as I said, raised white and have light skin, no one questioned my presence in the circle.

But that sensation needled me the rest of the weekend. Where do I belong? Is my Mexican identity considered legitimate by other Latinas? Would I be accepted by them as a Latina, or had I been too white for too long? The odd thing was that I had a few people of color pull me aside in the coming hours and ask me why I went downstairs. It was as if they were experiencing me as a fellow person of color, seeing my Mexican nature and not questioning me at all. The dissonance kept bouncing inside me.

The next morning was our final session together, and we celebrated mass with Richard Rohr and Alexie Torres. I welcomed the liturgy of my mother church and the blessings from my Latina sister. But the tension continued to build in me from the greeting to the final benediction. Once mass ended, I made my way to Alexie and poured out my heart. I told her about my Mexican birth mother, my adoption into whiteness, and that moment of not knowing where I belonged. I might have said something like, "I wasn't sure if you wanted me in your circle, so I went downstairs."

Alexie put her hands on my shoulders. "You are Mexican because of your mother. No one can take that from you. It is part of your story." Then she pulled me in close and said, "You are my *hermana*." At which point I began to sob. She named me sister. She said I irrevocably belonged to these women. She gave me permission to stand in solidarity with my Latina sisters and join the messy struggle of identity negotiation with them, not apart from them. My *hermana* spoke liberation into my spirit, because our freedom is connected to our true identity.

As an adopted person, I understand Moses, working to discern his dual identity. I appreciate Bithiah for doing her best to help him know who he was, both Hebrew and Egyptian. And I see how Jochebed remained present, nature coming to full fruition in her son over time. This is my own story as a daughter of two mothers, a woman navigating the intersection of nature and nurture. But glory be for the sisters, my *hermanas*, like Ada María Isasi-Díaz and Alexie Torres, who welcomed me home. They understood I could not travel the terrain alone and freed me to walk in a fuller experience of my own identity. It was another set of sisters that helped Moses see where true solidarity could be found. Maybe they delivered him too.

• • •

Underneath patriarchy reside strong and skilled women. More often than not, we work together. When necessary, we stand against harassers—be they shepherds or male-shaped government policies that impinge upon our work and our safety. We also stand together to support and celebrate one another, our accomplishments visible within the sisterhood.

But sisterhood moves toward solidarity when we are willing to listen deeply to the stories of our sisters who've been hurt by injustice—even injustice we've benefited from in some way. Our hearing and their healing are interconnected. We begin to see ways we've participated in the injustice, then we repent and unlearn our inherited ways. We commit to walk with our sisters, putting down our swords and spears and refashioning them into ploughs and pruning hooks so that we can work the fields together, then gather and feast. The shared work of solidarity is an embodiment of shalom.

"I believe the building of a new order of relationship, based in mutuality, is at the core of women's liberation," Ada María Isasi-Díaz writes in her seminal work, *Mujerista Theology*.[13] I believe her. A new order of relationship is what we see in the *SheLoves* sisters and Batwa women as they work to dismantle injustice in the world but also within their own friendships. They are creating a new order in the ways they stand with other women still suffering the effects of various oppressions. This new order recognizes *ubuntu*—that we are healed together, we know our identity more truly together, and we grow stronger as we work the fields together.

Moses grew, shaped by the embodied solidarity of his mother, Bithiah. She never forgot Jochebed and she never let Moses forget his Hebrew identity. He returned to the brickyards to see his kin—maybe he was looking for some tangible sense of solidarity for himself after years in a royal household. Witnessing the Egyptian and Hebrew at each other's throats would have been no surprise. But seeing embattled kinsmen where he expected solidarity must have knocked the wind out of him. It would be out of Egypt and across the desert where he would see the next expression of solidarity—in the seven sisters of Midian. Their work ethic and their capacity to function together in a man's world impressed him around the dinner table that first night, and all the nights after. They were his next school of solidarity, teaching him another necessary element of liberation.

Sometimes we don't see our own strength as clearly, though. In his poem "The State," Tamim Al-Barghouti offers a stunning allegory.[14] "A hyena attacks a herd of deer," he begins. The hyena picks one and lunges. But, he notes, "If the herd / Runs, not from her, but towards her / They crush her, bone and all." His observation, that the deer working in unison could defeat the predator, immediately brings to mind the possibilities of solidarity. But he moves beyond the simple to the more complex reality: "I also believe the herd is aware of its abilities / Yet each doe fears she'll be abandoned by her sisters / If she runs at the common foe." Riddled with doubt, each doe is alone in the moment of confrontation. We know we are strong together, but can we trust one another? This is the question solidarity asks.

I believe we can defy the stereotype of women as petty and competitive. I believe that together, we can defy the pharaohs of our day. But it will require us to trust one another during long and slow years, in moments when risk looms, and fear is at its peak. But if we learn from the sisters of Midian, like Moses did, we can be like the deer that trample the hyena of injustice.

Chapter 8

ZIPPORAH

Freedom through Sacrament

The days that followed the well incident sped by like a whirlwind. A chance meeting at the well became a dinner invitation; a meal became a marriage arrangement. There was scant conversation about the match, as good men like Moses don't travel through Midian often, much less men who are willing to stay and make it home. The wedding ceremony made Zipporah a wife and, soon enough, a mother.[1]

Not too long ago, she kept hours with the sun and her sisters tending the herd for their father. Clusters of sheep filled her daily horizon. Zipporah often sat with the laboring ewes, soothing them as they panted in the final phase of delivery— and no one showed more skill than her when a lamb was in distress and needed a quick intervention. Her hands were swift and steady under pressure, saving many ewes and lambs alike. Sometimes she missed the shoulder-to-shoulder work; it was backbreaking, but she knew every sister's every story. Now she stayed back in the compound shepherding her son. She was still strong, but softer round the edges.

If her days were filled with her son, then her nights were full of Moses. Her husband entered the tent tired, now more leathered by the sun since he replaced her as lead shepherd. He'd lie next to her and talk about the work, often asking questions since he hadn't herded sheep in Egypt. Unlike so many other men she knew, he listened well. She credited his mother and hoped she could raise her son with a similar sensibility. Zipporah tended to his intimate needs, allowing her hands to both soothe and stimulate. She tried to discern the nature of his knots—a product of his current Midian days or his past Egyptian ones? Moses tossed and turned most nights. If only she had a tincture to settle his soul.

Less time spent wrangling livestock created more time for Zipporah to study traditional medicine, a field whose practical wisdom was handed down by the women of her clan. She listened to the elder women as they performed various rituals, and she committed their words to memory. It was her father, a priest of Midian, who taught her to handle a flint, to balance its weight in her hand. Making a clean cut with what was essentially a stone took practice. She dedicated herself to mastering the sharp edge of the flint. Her strong grip and steady hand served her well. She observed the herbs used to calm rashes, ease muscle tension, reduce pain, and combat sleeplessness. She knew soon enough which leaves healed and which were set aside to hallow spaces. The line between the two was thin, but Zipporah possessed razor-sharp discernment. In her tent she was wife, mother, and priestess. Her husband admired her spiritual prowess and appreciated the prayers that kept their family safe. Together, he figured, they could thwart the evil of shepherds and spirits.

•   •   •

For many months she had been following the rabbi. She had heard him tell many of his parables—some more than once. She listened to his teachings on hillsides in Galilee and in Martha and Mary's home and witnessed multiple healings. She walked so close behind him that the dust kicked up by his feet would often cake her garments. She knew where he was headed because he said so on more than one occasion and in more than one way.

One evening, she left her house for a dinner party at her neighbor Simon's, where the rabbi would be in attendance. She brought with her a small alabaster jar of high-quality nard, which she had recently saved up for and purchased.

By the time she arrived, the rabbi was already there. He was sitting at the table and laughing with Simon, once a leper, and some other friends. The twelve disciples were mingling about the room in spirited conversation while the house staff brought platters of food and began pouring the wine.

Now is the time, she thought. She took a deep breath and felt the weight of the jar in her calloused hand. She walked toward the rabbi. She broke open the top of the jar and began to pour the ointment over his coarse, dark hair, hair that reminded her of her own brother's. But unlike her brother, the rabbi was destined not just for death but for victory too. In her bones she knew him to be Messiah, though she hardly could conceive of what that really meant. She poured slowly . . . pondering these things.

She was remembering how her mother poured the oil over her brother's young, dead body when Peter's sharp elbow jolted her, followed by the angry words of Judas. The room was filled with noise, with shouting, with accusation. She was confused. Didn't they all know what she was doing? Hadn't they seen their mothers prepare bodies before? But they did not see what she saw or know what she knew.

But the rabbi knew. He felt the cool ointment dripping down his scalp and neck—and knew the fragrance immediately. She was preparing him for what lay ahead—martyrdom—and making visible his salvific purpose.

He pushed back Peter and the others pressing toward her, and he chided Judas with one sharp look. Like Moses at the well, he delivered the woman from the overly aggressive men. Then he spoke, "She has anointed me." The woman sighed in deep relief as she realized that the rabbi had received her sacramental gesture.

Like the prophets of old who anointed leaders in Israel, this woman anointed Jesus, proclaiming his true identity. It was she who stood in the long prophetic tradition alongside John the Baptist, baptizing Jesus into his identity—not Peter, who attempted to announce him as Messiah but then misunderstood his agenda entirely. It was she who was the perceptive prophet and sacramental practitioner, knowing how to anoint. She *messiahed* Jesus.[2]

She possessed an insight cultivated over months of patient watching, listening, and pondering. She invested in the ointment of nard and made an intentional decision to take it with her on that cool night. She was inspired by the Spirit to anoint and therefore participate in the work of Jesus, giving momentum to his salvation agenda. One scholar notes that she *empowered* him, the disciple empowering the rabbi.[3] What a stunning reversal!

This story lives in what Emmanuel Katongole[4] calls the Bethany narratives. These Gospel stories tell of Jesus's time in Bethany, a small village not too far from Jerusalem. Here is where we meet Martha and Mary, sisters of Lazarus. Here is where healings happened—even a resurrection. And here is where an unnamed follower of the rabbi anointed his head with aromatic nard, signaling his time was coming.

I remember sitting in the grassy side yard in a white plastic chair at Father Katongole's guesthouse in Entebbe, Uganda. He led us through the Bethany narratives for a theological intensive hosted by Amahoro Africa, a network of African leaders. He cracked open Matthew 26 and read this passage to us. Here, I thought, was a woman who knew what the moment demanded. She saved coins, procured high-quality nard, and let it sit on her bedside table. And waited. Jesus came and went through Bethany many times, visiting his dear friends, the trio of siblings. But she intuited that this was the night to bring the alabaster jar. She knew the logistics of anointing, so she came ready. There was nothing haphazard about her extravagant ritual. Like Zipporah with her flint, as we will see below, she was prepared to step into the propitious moment and perform the sacrament. Her reward, not that she sought one, was that she'd be remembered as long as the story of the night was told across the generations. The ritual she enacted allowed Jesus to move forward into the vocation awaiting him in Jerusalem, much like Zipporah's circumcising intervention allowed Moses to proceed to Egypt to fulfill his liberation vocation.

The men in our circle seemed to shift from side to side in their chairs. Maybe they saw more like the men in Simon's house that night and felt the discomfort of it. They thought she was seeking forgiveness for something, maybe prostitution, or perhaps making a show of her submission to the rabbi. They were reluctant to call her a prophet. But the women in our group were clear-eyed as they viewed this sister from Bethany. This woman knew what the rabbi needed to make it to Jerusalem, and she performed the ritual masterfully. We women homed in on the sacrament, not the scandal, of the woman.

The next day would be our final one together in Uganda. I wanted to mark the final session. I asked Father Katongole if he would preside over Communion. He let me know that Communion was off the table because we were a mixed group of Catholics and Protestants. There is a priestly protocol to such holy gestures, and this pulled him too close to the edge of overstepping. "What about anointing us with a cross on our foreheads?" I asked. As a Catholic priest, he said, he could not just anoint people's heads willy-nilly. It seemed every sacred rite I mentioned, he countered with a reason why church etiquette would not allow it.

I was undeterred. I knew we needed a communal, sacramental moment to seal our time together. "What if we anointed one another's feet with oil? It's not anointing of foreheads, and it's not foot washing. It is something different for this time, this place, and these people." Father Katongole had no hesitation about this gesture and willingly joined me in putting our plan in place for the final session.

There were twenty of us ringed around the living room, seated in armchairs and on couches. I began by reading the Bethany story from Mark's Gospel this time—same story, different storyteller. Then, the anointing. I went first, kneeling in front of the person to my right. I dipped my finger into a small ceramic bowl of olive oil from the kitchen and made the sign of the cross on both her feet. As I did, I offered simple words of blessing for these feet and this friend. Each person followed suit around the circle. At last it was time for Father Katongole to anoint my feet—cracked heels, chipped polish, and all. He bent before me in a slow bow, dragging the oil across my feet in a large cross. He blessed me with words I can't recite, but his tears I will never forget. It was holy.

Later as we all said our goodbyes, Father Katongole thanked me for the idea of anointing feet. It allowed us to share a sacramental moment together as brothers and sisters in Christ, with an appropriate nod to our sister from Bethany. It moved us beyond our denominational lines to a common ground. He was right: too often our traditions cordon us off from experiencing sacraments together across tribal lines. It would have been easy to exhaust the ones known to us and then give up. But my insistence was rewarded. There was a rite we created together, a way to hallow shared space. This is how women hold sacrament. It is not mere ritual but a way to honor thin places where humanity and the Holy meet.

●　　　●　　　●

Midian was a man's world—and it was nothing without the love of a woman, Moses learned. While patriarchy moved women like commodities to create connections and ensure solidarity between clans, it didn't completely define a woman's contribution to the family. Zipporah, a wife and mother, was also a partner and priestess of their home. Moses knew he had found a capable wife in Zipporah, a woman who did not let the lamp go out at night.[5] She was, in many ways, a hedge of protection around her family.

Women worked hard to help build and sustain their communities.[6] Contrary to our assumptions about biblical times, their labor wasn't limited to domestic tasks associated with the kitchen or child-rearing only. When male energies were usurped by large construction projects like cisterns, terraced fields, or other communal infrastructure projects, women stepped in to cover what remained. This meant that alongside the traditional tasks we associate with women, they also worked the fields, shepherded flocks, and labored hard to maintain the homestead.

In addition to carrying out the more common domestic work, women were priests in the home—the people who knew the rituals and presided over sacred rites within the family.[7] It was not uncommon for women to perform circumcisions, create tinctures to bring health or encourage pregnancy (remember Leah's mandrakes?[8]), and perform other rituals to enact blessings or, more often, ward off evil. Lamps were lit not only for light but also in prayer and often as a sign of protection against menaces in the night.[9] Men were the priests of public spaces with more nationalistic concerns, but women mediated the rituals of faith in the home day to day.[10] Women employed their full heart, mind, and strength to the service of their family; this included their sacramental sensibilities.

Moses met Zipporah while she tended the family herd, noticing her physical strength and strategic capacity. Once married, he no doubt knew her as lover and soon after witnessed her as mother. She would have kept a garden and made meals, created a suitable home for their family within her father's compound. And as the daughter of a priest, she certainly learned the rituals of their religion—maybe more than most. She naturally observed the wise women of the clan, studying their ways of healing bodies and hallowing space. Within her home, she was a sacramental practitioner. When it came to blessings, Moses counted Zipporah first among many. She kept their home, made it function, and even consecrated it with her priestly ways. She was not only a blessing but also one who knew how to bless. She kept the lamp burning so that all slept safe under her roof.

•   •   •

Idelette and I dreamed of hosting the *SheLoves Magazine* readers and writers for a retreat, and one February weekend it happened in the mountain town of Chilliwack, British Columbia. We cracked open our friendship and invited our sisters into our favorite conversations about Jesus, justice, and what it looks like to see women rising. I looked across the landscape of women and saw through Idelette's eyes the Holy Grail, cupped in the hands of Jesus and poured out as a blessing.

Melaney G. Lyall, an Indigenous sister from the Musqueam Indian Band, opened our gathering with a traditional welcome song on Thursday night. She located us in a place, reminding us of a people who inhabited the land first. Kallie Wood, a Nakoda Cree of Carry the Kettle First Nation, also joined us. Throughout the weekend, a weaving began among us, Indigenous and not. Songs, stories, and sacraments invited us to recognize the suffering of our Indigenous sisters and the weight their communities carried in the world. Idelette and I knew it was important to include Melaney and Kallie in our gathering, but I think what happened surprised even us.

During our time together, we shared our stories. We were new mothers, immigrants, brown women in white-dominated spaces, and empty-nesters wondering about what the next season held for us. We came confident, excited, shy, scared, and hungry. We took risks to break open our lives with one another and trust our words would find welcome. I lit a candle to honor Mother Mary and my Mexican sisters before I opened the book of Exodus and exhorted our women to be "Exodus strong." These women—Shiphrah, Puah, Jochebed, Bithiah, and Miriam—created the conditions for liberation. And we, in a post-election world riddled with xenophobia and fear, could join them in liberation work.

Melaney invited us to join her in a small outdoor amphitheater, in the cold, to enter into the mystery her Musqueam siblings stewarded all these years. She offered prayers. She sang songs handed down by generations, allowing us to participate in something ancient and true. She taught us about blanketing, the practice of draping someone with a large scarf or blanket across their shoulders to honor them and affix a blessing to them. Her willingness to perform sacred rites with us wove us more tightly together. This was not a scheduled part of the event but something she sensed the women were ready for, and so she stepped into the moment as a skilled spiritual practitioner. She intuitively knew what was required to move us into deeper regions of connection.

While we were together, there was a loss in Kallie's Nakoda Cree community back in Regina, Saskatchewan. She stood in front of our room and lit a candle to remember the young man who took his life overnight. He was the fourth in so many weeks. We watched the candle flicker and held the silence. We prayed for Kallie, the young man's family, and their community. We tried to imagine together what the New City vision of Isaiah would look like in her community, where no Indigenous youth would fall prey to suicide because they would know justice, purpose, and the strength of their tradition. They would be able to hold their heads up high on their ancestors' land, knowing both their tribal language and their traditions. Our communal lament and imagining that morning created space to feel the ache and pray through it together. Silence, tears, and hope mingled together. Again, we breached the shallow space and pushed toward deeper territory.

Fiona, who traveled from her home and children in England to be with us, told us how she was learning about God as Mother.

One way she was doing this was by singing hymns and spirituals, replacing the masculine pronouns for God with feminine ones. So Fiona sang in a small and beautiful voice, "She's got the whole world in Her hands, She's got the whole world in Her hands . . . ," and we joined in. We created new verses. "She's got the immigrant and refugee in Her hands, She's got the mamas and their babies in Her hands," and we ended in unison: "She's got you and me, sister, in Her hands; She's got the whole world in Her hands." The song was strong and gentle at the same time, seeping into the crevices of our collective soul. Ever since Fiona first sang, I have been able to experience God as Mother in a way I never imagined before. Fiona created a sacred rite that enabled me to access an aspect of God in a new and holy way. This is what true sacramental practitioners do.

Idelette, Kallie, Melaney, and I watched as the weekend progressed and the women continued to be knit closer together. So much of what transpired between us lived in the spaces between story and sacrament as we mediated God's goodness to one another. So many women brought practices from their own homes and daily lives that became sacraments. We were practitioners of the holy.

By the time we reached Sunday morning, it felt as if the four of us were leading shoulder to shoulder, like four points of the compass coming together in a moment of convergence. The culmination of our weekend conversation was a time of communion. I preached. Idelette prayed over the bread and wine. We offered the women the bread of *amahoro* and the wine of *ubuntu* in recognition of the peace and interconnection between us.[11] Once the women took the elements, they moved toward Kallie and Melaney, who blanketed each woman with an Indigenous scarf as a blessing. The four of us administered the sacraments together seamlessly.

We ended our time with one hundred women forming an unbroken circle against the wood-paneled walls of the meeting room. Melaney stood in the center with her hand drum. She sang again. Her voice was deeper, richer, and somehow rounder than before. There was an undeniable strength in her drumming. It was the same song from our first night together, but now her song resonated in us. We were part of the song, and together our sound was a sacrament that echoed with Spirit.

•   •   •

Decades go by. Zipporah has a second son. Moses shepherds the herds and settles in Midian and into family life. One day he sees a bush aflame and stops to *really* see it. The bush burns but doesn't collapse into ash. It just burns with a hot Presence. And the Presence calls him home—to participate in the deliverance of his kin. So Moses, with his father-in-law's blessing, packs up Zipporah and their boys and begins the journey back to Egypt.

On the way, the family stops for the night. God meets him and is on the verge of killing him. Zipporah, alert in the darkness, reaches for her ritual flint with one hand and her infant son with the other. She circumcises her boy. She takes the foreskin and touches Moses—maybe his feet, maybe his genitals. She calls Moses a "bridegroom of blood to me." And with that pronouncement, God leaves him alone.[12]

In this enigmatic passage, the action comes fast. God finds Moses in the night and is more dangerous than any wild animal, lest we think God is ever tame or predictable. God has Moses within reach . . . but Zipporah intervenes. In the moment, she knows exactly what is needed to appease God and send the Hunter away. She performs the ritual. What is ambiguous to us—the exact rite, what part of Moses makes contact with the cut skin, what her declaration means—is clear to her. She performs the rite without hesitation, without a hint of fear.[13] As a skilled sacramental practitioner, she discerns the moment rightly. She saves Moses's life.

Maybe we stand aghast at a murderous God, unable to square Love with death. But Zipporah was not surprised; she was prepared. She birthed two children and served as midwife to countless others; she knew how precarious life was, how thin the line between a blessing and a curse. As one well versed in sacramental work, she understood that while God is steadfast, God is not safe. Prayers and rituals open us to the Holy One, but there are no guarantees with any rite or for any practitioner—not even the chosen liberator en route to Egypt. So we enter Zipporah's space, where God is good and worthy of our attention. But none of us are ever safe when the Holy Hunter is roaming the night—so we watch, we pray, and we live ready to perform sacraments that save lives.

Here again is a woman saving Moses. Zipporah follows the midwives, Jochebed, Miriam, and Bithiah in small acts of defiance, nurture, and sacrament that prove salvific for this would-be liberator. He would not have survived the Nile River, the brickyards of Egypt, or the darkened desert without Exodus-strong women. Each woman delivered Moses so that he could step into his vocation and deliver the Hebrews from slavery.

This passage in Exodus is part of a larger section that focuses on Moses's call and vocation. While I see the narrator's purpose, I come to the narrative from a different angle. I look at Zipporah. Once a shepherdess, then a wife and a mother, she found her vocation in administering the sacraments. She learned, she practiced. She honed her flint-wielding skills and her discernment. She operated in her calling as a priestess, a practitioner of the holy. In an extreme moment of testing in the darkness of a desert night, she reached the pinnacle of her vocation as she thwarted the Dangerous Divine One and saved Moses. We never hear the details of her call, but we see her live it out nonetheless. The narrator, because his focus is on Moses, is matter-of-fact about Zipporah. It would be easy to miss her significance. But she shone as Moses would one future day when he would lead the people across the Reed Sea. One day Moses would embody his vocation as Zipporah did hers that night.

·　　　·　　　·

In the darkest part of the night, his feet skated across the cold tile floor until he stood, teetering and breathless, by my bed: "Mama, I had a bad dream." Even through the blackness I could see his eyes, glazed with fear and lingering tendrils of sleep.

I sat up in bed. I took his small hand in mine, looked him in the eye, and invited him to take a deep breath with me. In the span between our slow inhale and exhale, he shook the nightmare's hold.

"You're all right, Justin. *You are awake and safe at home with me.* Emma's all right—she's sleeping in her room. Papa's OK too." He nodded slowly, registering the truths I'd just spoken into the night air between us. I made the sign of the cross on his forehead. I told him he could return to bed because all is well; we're all safe. He shuffled down the hall and burrowed back under his blankets. The nightmare came to an end, the monsters banished to another realm far away.

Every time I hear those fast-moving feet approaching, I prepare to give a salvation oracle to my son. I wake him up to the reality that he isn't under threat anymore but safe in my room where night terrors possess no power to hurt him. My singular goal in that midnight moment: make sure he knows he's safe. Once he understands what's real, the menacing phantoms in his room are unmasked, no longer real and no longer scary.

I owe this bit of wisdom to Walter Brueggemann, who wrote somewhere that a salvation oracle is meant to break the power of nightmares by reminding us that all is well. I think I took the advice a bit more literally than he intended, but salvation oracles are how we confront and dismantle nightmares in our house now.

When presented with the opportunity to move to Burundi, I feared leaving my job, my house, and the world I knew. My circle of women gathered around me and spoke in unison: *Don't be afraid, God is in this, He is with you as you go.* They stood around me, hands on my shoulders, on my back, one even holding my hands. They prayed blessings for me. They gave me the courage to quit my job and go to Burundi. They stood against the monsters threatening me and enacted a salvation oracle, setting me free.[14]

Salvation oracles speak of safety, but also of presence and proximity. They are sacraments we speak to one another—sometimes bedside to dispel terrors of the night, and other times in the brightness of day, where fear can blind us and hold us captive. Women are especially adept at pronouncing such oracles, offering deliverances small and large to those in their orbit.

◆　　　◆　　　◆

Our work is so often called magic—anointing feet, burning incense, lighting candles, and other rituals. Especially as a woman with Mexican blood flowing through my *corazón*, these rituals are the stuff of my daily practice of faith. Too often such work isn't recognized by the religious elite because it happens at home, as informal as a spontaneous prayer or the striking of a match. Some of us are credentialed these days—educated in seminaries and ordained by denominations, set apart to minister in official spaces. Many of us practice our sacraments at home among family and friends, maybe even among our neighbors. But either way, women are practitioners of the sacraments in life-giving, even life-saving, ways. It is part of how we contribute to liberation.

Chapter 9

THE NILE NETWORK

Freedom through Neighborliness

The Nile network ebbed and flowed like the river itself. For many seasons the women worked furiously, criss-crossing the water to save lives and support one another when pharaonic forces heightened. At other times the alliance of women seemed more staid, the mothers lulled into a stupor of hopelessness. The long arc of liberation bent slowly for those suffering under the oppression of one pharaoh or another. Yet women persevered, their strength revealed in decades of stamina and patience.

One constant in the resistance movement was a network built on neighborliness. Women reached out to one another and cultivated deep relationships to sustain them through the years of oppression. No one can survive systemic dehumanization alone. Out of both nature and necessity, the Hebrew women banded together in the shadow of the brickyards. This, however, was not an exclusivist endeavor. The network functioned as a bridge between the women on both sides of the river, who were connected in salvific work that required trust, mutuality, and hope. Miriam and her mother may have been the first to cross over and establish a crucial connection with Pharaoh's daughter, but it was only the beginning of women seeing themselves as allies. Extreme duress pushed the Hebrew and Egyptian daughters to embody a solidarity that would erode the empire.

After desperation drew mothers around a crying Hebrew boy, the women grew in friendship over years of shared resistance. How could it be otherwise? They were in each other's homes. At times their meetings were clandestine, and the secrecy pressed them to lean in and trust one another. Other times they met up in places far enough out of sight that they laughed loudly, letting their guard down in mixed company. Bithiah learned how to spot possible allies within the imperial compound and elite streets of the capital. Miriam, now a young woman, was a twin force on the Nile's backside, convincing women that there were Egyptians with compassion and even means to assist them. The network grew as if by capillary action, never resting.

It would be easy to assume Hebrew women lived only on one side of the river and Egyptians on the other. While this might have been partly true, spaces existed where their residences overlapped.[1] Some enslaved women lived in service to imperial households, sleeping under the same tiled roof as their mistresses. A good many streets were likely mixed, as working-class Egyptians lived in close proximity to Hebrew laborers. Neighborhoods brought women into natural contact with each other. Women who lived next door and those across the river became partners in good trouble.[2]

◆　　　◆　　　◆

"Can this be Naomi?" the women of Bethlehem exclaimed. Naomi left Bethlehem as a young wife with her husband to escape a famine and find refuge in Moab. She reentered her homeland as a widow deprived of even her sons. All she possessed was a Moabite daughter-in-law named Ruth, who pledged allegiance to her and to the God of Israel. Once she was full; now she returned empty. All sweetness soured into bitterness.[3] The townswomen gathered round her to listen and lament. The network of women quickly activated on behalf of Naomi, standing in solidarity with their long-lost neighbor.[4]

Naomi and Ruth survived on the edge of the community. Ruth gleaned grain on a nearby farm, demonstrating the two women's continued food insecurity, even after Bethlehem's famine had passed. Through a series of bold moves, the women worked in tandem to secure redemption. At the narrative's end, the women of Bethlehem are still with Ruth and Naomi, having witnessed it all.

Ruth births a son, though it sounds as if Naomi will be a mother to him, as he restores her claim to her husband's ancestral land. Naomi's neighbors saw the boy and celebrated: "Praise God, who is redeeming and sustaining you!" They not only shared in her joy; they joined her in naming the child.[5] The community of women embraced Naomi's resurrection. Her arms, once empty, now hold a son, a future, and a new life.

It would be easy to miss Naomi's neighbors; indeed, Scripture often does overlook such networks of women.[6] But this is not the first time we see women of the neighborhood at work. Worth our notice is that the feminine noun for *neighbor* is used only twice in the Hebrew Bible: to speak of Naomi's neighbors, and to speak of the Hebrew women's Egyptian neighbors.[7] In both cases we catch a glimpse of neighborhood women who created informal networks to support one another and affirm life. They functioned as the connective tissue of the community.

•   •   •

The women in Egypt also formed local alliances for support and action.[8] I imagine they cultivated genuine affection for their Hebrew neighbors over time, traversing the same streets, frequenting the same markets, and gathering round the same wells. Their relationships became the seed for future liberation for oppressor and oppressed alike.

While Pharaoh's bellicose language reverberated throughout the land, women quietly convened with their would-be enemies, creating connections. While his death order for male infants remained in effect, women daily defied it as neighbors who knew each other, and who thus knew better than to threaten their neighbors' sons. They dismantled hostilities through neighborliness. Beneath the text and woven throughout most societies are networks of women working to safeguard the families within the community, collectively thwarting whatever injustice weighs upon them. There is goodness in the informal neighborly networks of women. This, too, is a vital and vibrant part of liberation practice.

When I zoom in tight on the Nile network, I see the instances of collaboration among the various women. I imagine there were more women involved in the resistance than is detailed by the narrator of Exodus. But when we take a wider shot of the landscape, we see the larger reality that many Egyptian women were content to be beneficiaries of Pharaoh's system. They assumed they had earned their life of ease and the advantages they enjoyed. Most women were not part of the network; they remained comfortably complicit.

Exodus is a masterful work of imagination. The narrative provides plenty of room to see what is possible on both sides of the river. But we can still see what is and lament that too many women stayed cocooned in their privilege, in whatever measure they possessed it, rather than risking engagement. Maybe many of the Egyptians did not get close to mixed neighborhoods and had no opportunity to befriend Hebrew women. Maybe the intentionality it would have required was more than they were willing to invest, and so they did not become members of the Nile network or even neighbors. Some women could choose to circulate in different orbits from those who suffered under the pharaonic policies and so never put their privilege to good use on behalf of others.

Sadly, this is still too true today. Though there is a Nile network—and it is growing—far too many women navigate away from the fray when they encounter inconvenient truths that might upend their way of life. They stay in their gated communities and marvel at the pyramids and storehouses from afar. Nothing is new under the sun.

•   •   •

Moses stood barefoot at the burning bush for quite some time; God had much to say. God called him to return to Egypt to save his kin, declared an enigmatic Name, and promised that Moses would witness God's favor as he watched Hebrews plunder Egypt.[9] All of this was intended to fortify Moses for the long walk to freedom that lay ahead.

The prophetic word about plunder resurrected God's covenantal promise to Abraham: there will be four hundred years of enslavement in a foreign land, but upon emancipation, Abraham's descendants will leave with many possessions.[10] In the conversation at the blazing bush, the possessions are detailed as jewelry of silver and gold, even clothing, that the women will receive from their neighbors on the way out of Egypt. Moses is embarking on an epic journey, but again, it appears that the women precede him in creating the conditions for liberation. What we learn as we eavesdrop is that the Hebrew people will experience the favor of the Egyptians on their way out of slavery, a favor that will not let them leave empty-handed.[11]

God declared that favor would look like Hebrew women asking their neighbors for their treasured things, jewels and clothes, and Egyptian women giving their valuables without resistance.[12] This, God says, is how Egypt will be "plundered." The transfer of wealth begins with the Nile network living out neighborliness, which fosters goodwill, and then those relationships become the road for recompense. The women make a way where none could previously be seen or imagined.

The transfer of wealth through the hands of neighbors is predicted to occur a second time as well. In a final warning before the last plague, God tells Moses to be prepared for what is about to happen. God instructs Moses to tell the men to ask their neighbors, and the women to ask theirs, for silver, gold, and clothing.[13] Again there is the mention of favorable relations between them, so they can expect to receive what they request from their Egyptian neighbors. Here both women and men are put on notice that they can expect gifts from their neighbors as they make their way out of the house of bondage.

The final time the narrator speaks of neighbors, favor, and jewels, it's in the past tense, as God's prediction had come to pass. The angel of death visited Egypt in the dead of night, taking the lives of the firstborn Egyptians. Pharaoh begged the Hebrews to leave immediately. The Hebrews grabbed their unleavened bread—and asked their neighbors for clothes and jewelry on their way out of town, which the Egyptians willingly relinquished. That, the narrator reports, is how the Hebrews plundered Egypt.[14]

It's interesting, even instructive, that the first mention in this trio of interlinked passages specifically notes that the women pioneered this neighborly dynamic. Women are the prototype. But as we learn in the next mention, the men are similarly expected to forge neighborhood alliances. And finally, it is all Hebrews who live in favor with their Egyptian neighbors and walk out of the brickyards with booty. Women laid the groundwork, plundering the empire by acting like true neighbors.

The story told is one not of force but of favor. The relationships developed by the Hebrews over time with those in proximity to them provided a foundation for repair work. Neighbors were at ease with one another. Egyptians could believe the best about their neighbors, and the Hebrews could give theirs the benefit of the doubt. Maybe this is what favor looks like at first: the willingness to make connections with those different from us.

But when the final plague exacted its deadly due, everyone knew it was time for an exodus. Neighbors knocked on doors and asked for what they needed—or what was due them after generations of servitude. And they got what they asked for—gold and silver and clothes carried out on the backs of their children. The ease of the exchange might also be a glimpse of what favor can look like among true neighbors. Sustained relationships pave the way for wealth to move from Egyptian hands into Hebrew ones. The goods moved like gifts, with generosity and not violence. In short, favor looked like reparations.

•   •   •

Dalia Landau was born in Bulgaria in 1947 to parents who survived the Holocaust. With memories still hot as the ovens of Treblinka, her parents relinquished their Bulgarian passports and boarded a ship for Israel to start a new life in an ancient land in the summer of 1948. After spending weeks in an immigration camp, they found an empty home in the small town of Ramle to inhabit. The emerging Israeli government told the family that the Palestinian Arabs who once lived there just fled, leaving the home vacant. Papers were signed, and the house with the lemon tree in the courtyard was their new home in the land filled with promise.

This is where Dalia grew up. Her childhood memories are anchored in this house. It seldom occurred to her that another person could say the same. Until, in the aftermath of the 1967 Arab-Israeli War, three men came to her home. She laid eyes on them and intuitively knew why they were at her gate.[15]

When Bashir Khairi and his cousins entered the home, she would learn that his father built the home for his bride in 1936. Their family began here. They fled under duress in 1948, thinking it was a temporary displacement until the hostilities ended. By the summer of that same year, all the Palestinian Arabs were pushed out of Ramle for good. Bashir and his family relocated to Ramallah, in the now-occupied territory of the West Bank. Meeting Bashir broke Dalia's ignorance and cracked her complicity. "When she opened the door for Bashir, she opened the door into a whole new reality she had scarcely been aware of until then—the reality of the Palestinian Arabs living in her midst and the responsibility that she bore towards them."[16] Though Bashir and his cousins only intended to see their family home that day, their visit was a catalyst for Dalia.

At a later date, Dalia reached out to Bashir in the hope of establishing a connection. She visited his home in Ramallah intermittently over the next fifteen years. She wanted to understand more. Even when Bashir was in prison for a bombing in Israel (of which he maintains his innocence), she kept contact as best she could by sending letters. The shared house with the lemon tree in the yard became a tangible metaphor for their connection to the land and to each other.

The house in Ramle was Dalia's inheritance upon the death of her parents. She hoped to return the house to Bashir's family (it was as if the shofar sounded and the jubilee imperative pressed upon her[17]). Amends had to be made. But an unjust bureaucracy stood in her way. Since Bashir lived in the West Bank and was not an Israeli citizen, he was ineligible to own the property in Ramle. While the logistics of the land transfer impeded a true return of the land from Dalia's family back to Bashir's, Dalia kept insisting on Jubilee.

Since Dalia and her husband lived in Jerusalem, the inherited house could be repurposed in any number of ways. She offered to sell the house and give the funds to the Khairi family. Bashir didn't want the money. He countered with another idea entirely. He wanted their house to become a preschool for Arab children. Dalia agreed, and in 1991 the preschool opened along with Open House, a center for coexistence between Jews and Arabs run by Dalia. Bashir had since been deported to Lebanon, but the house turned preschool was his legacy.

Dalia clearly understood that reparations were in order. "I am part of the problem because I came from Europe, because I live in an Arab house. I am part of the solution, because I love."[18]

This is the voice of a neighbor who understands that she is part of the reparatory work of healing in her land. The mending she and Bashir attempted together may not be perfect, but it is a small gesture toward countering the pharaonic forces at work in Israel-Palestine.

·　　·　　·

Many commentators say the Exodus narrator speaks with irony about the giving of goods. When the word *plunder* is at last spoken, they claim it reveals the reality of the exchange. How could the movement of treasure be anything other than violent—a forced taking by slaves from their oppressors? They have a point. The other use of *plunder* in the Hebrew Bible is found in a battle narrative where the Israelites take no prisoners but take all the valuables of the vanquished in an act of outright theft.[19]

But I return to the coupling of *neighbors* and *favor*, and the repeated idea of goods given freely. Could it be that neighborly relations temper the dynamic of plunder? Could the favor that exists between friends change the meaning of *plunder* in these specific instances?

The same could apply to the economic practice of Jubilee, which commands the return of land and release of all slaves and all debts on the fiftieth year.[20] The return of land and debt relief is good news for the poor. However, it is hard news for those who stand to lose land and labor when the shofar sounds. It matters where you stand in the economy on the eve of the fiftieth year as to how you will hear the word of Jubilee. If the goods move toward you, it will feel like recompense for generations of enslavement. But if the goods move out of your house and into the hands of others, it might feel like the sting of plunder.

Another way to understand the use of *plunder* in this narrative is as hyperbole.[21] The Hebrews leave with just compensation for their labor. But one person's compensation is another's plunder. And while the transfer of treasure may have happened through the kindness of neighbors, to some the loss itself was violent. The narrator wants us to see that wealth was redistributed in dramatic fashion. It is the language of defeat for Pharaoh and his regime. Pharaoh was the most plundered of all—losing his son, his labor force, and his empire's entire wealth. But to say that the Hebrews plundered the Egyptians literally is to exaggerate and miss the crux of the story.

In this interpretive moment we imagine Egypt letting go, emancipation happening with order and a degree of recompense.[22] The enslaved go out with seed money to build a new life (or a tabernacle, in their case), and those once complicit in the predatory regime make efforts toward amends. In these acts of good faith and restitution, all find hope for collective healing. All are set free.

·   ·   ·

It sounds unrealistic that enemies would be neighbors; it's impossible to think that Egyptians gave away their wealth freely. Yet this is what God dares us to envision as the story unfolds: wealth transferred through the hands of neighbors to rectify an injustice they both acknowledge. The women lead the way, and the men aren't exempt from following their example. God's favor empowered neighborly relations so that reparations could happen hand in hand with emancipation.

Dalia's reparatory gesture tells me to keep an open mind—reparations can happen. I heard a story from the Canadian West about a faithful Mennonite woman who recognized that she was living on stolen land. She learned that while her government now made provision for Indigenous people to buy back their land when it became available for sale, even extending them first rights on such purchases, many could not afford it. This lack of financial power to purchase property even when under optimal circumstances was part of years of intergenerational injustice. Having learned about her Indigenous neighbors and befriending them, the Mennonite woman decided to do the one small thing she could: rewrite her will. She decided to transfer a substantial sum of her inheritance to a fund for her Indigenous neighbors. The next time land became available for purchase, they could use her inheritance to reclaim it. Reparations still happen between neighbors.

My friend Paige lives in a row house in Philadelphia. She is raising her white family in an African American neighborhood in order to embody intentional neighborliness. Living among the black community, she is learning how to dismantle her privilege, see injustice, and walk in solidarity with her neighbors. She told me how the families around her love that her white family rents from an African American owner, the reverse of too many of their stories. Sharing in the challenges of the street as well as in the sweetness of porch life together in the warmer months has allowed these families to forge true bonds of friendship. Paige told me she wants to settle here, that this is not a temporary placement. For her this means someday owning a home, maybe even this very one if the owner ever wants to sell. "But," she mused, "I would need to consult with my neighbors. Maybe they don't want us to own, to become another white owner on this predominantly black street. It might matter to them, and so it matters to us. I could not buy if it would hurt our neighbors." And right there is the seed of reparations in the heart of a true neighbor. Paige is already considering how purchasing a home might impinge upon her neighbors, and wants to keep them in mind as she thinks about the long trajectory of their street.

Another friend recently told me about college funds for her two young daughters. "We are thinking of starting a third fund," she said. Not because they are planning on a third child, but because this might be a small act of reparation they can do for another family, recognizing the injustice of slavery and resulting imbalance of resources. If they contribute monthly to three college funds, sometime in the future they could cede the third account to an African American family who could not save for their child's college education because they worked all those years to survive. This family is working reparation into their financial planning, trusting that it will happen.

What if neighborly relations prepare the way for reparations? Could it be that when our hearts turn toward one another and we see injustice and the cost it exacts, we might even recognize our own complicity and seek to right the wrong? Giving our goods to our neighbors becomes recognition of the wrongs done and suffered. The divestment becomes a way to begin restoration for oppressed and oppressor alike. The former Hebrew slaves leave with seed for their emancipated life outside Egypt— with the means to begin again—while the oppressor, through reparative giving, is freed from the chokehold of complicity.

◆　　◆　　◆

Danielle aspires to nothing more than to live as a good neighbor. A self-proclaimed failed missionary, she now channels her energies into God's imperatives regarding neighbor love. She and her family live on the outskirts of Portland, Oregon, in a community populated by resettled refugees from the world's most painful places.

Initially Danielle moved into Barberry Village, a low-income apartment complex on a street with no sidewalks. Her back porch, a simple cement pad, opened up to the courtyard where Somali mamas, Cuban grandmas, Iraqi men, and Syrian children passed by. She'd sit on her turquoise plastic chair and watch her kids play with neighbor kids while their parents kept to themselves. But month by month, the women began to visit. Conversations began. Stories and meals were shared. Some even accepted her invitation to holiday meals and ventured into their first American home, less sure about the turkey and sides but always eager for Danielle's homemade cake and plenty of soda. These were neighbors who knew and cared for one another.

Danielle also received their hospitality and entered their apartments. Over plates of Afghani food eaten on sunk-in secondhand couches, Danielle listened and laughed in turn. Here is where she learned about the hardship suffered by her friends as they fled homes turned into conflict zones, leaving behind family members they'll likely never see again, and landed in refugee camps that introduced another kind of trauma into their story. They arrived in America with hopes of sleeping safely through the night and seeing their children grow up healthy and strong. But the hospitality was incomplete. They were relegated to low-income housing and under-resourced schools and were often targets for predatory landlords, not to mention the ever-rolling wave of gentrification that threatened their place in the neighborhood. Knowing all this, now it was Danielle who wasn't sleeping through the night.

Danielle and her family decided to make their presence in the community permanent. They found a house just around the corner from Barberry Village that sits on the street between the apartment complex and the elementary school. All the neighbors would pass by daily as they walked their kids to and from school. Often Danielle and her daughter would walk with them. In a series of small moves, Danielle kept choosing her neighbors and a life lived in solidarity with them.

There was one park in the neighborhood. It was the one place within walking distance from the Barberry compound where kids could run and play while the mamas sat in the fresh air and maybe caught a slice of sun through the Portland gray sky. Danielle was there with her kids swinging on the weathered swing set when she noticed an official placard posted by the city announcing the plan to relocate the park. The plot was slated for redevelopment into something unusable by her neighbors. The park would be moved to a place their feet could not reasonably take them. The entire community would lose the only common space available to them. Her neighbors just shrugged, another loss they were powerless to fight.

It took only a few days of stewing before Danielle began making inquiries. She called city council members and asked questions. She called other advocates across the city for guidance. She wrote a few articles in local papers. She summoned the courage to attend her first-ever city council meeting and speak up. She talked about what the park meant to this community and refused to accept development plans that left her neighbors out. She made just enough noise to make a small difference. I watched her over the months and witnessed a true neighbor laboring with such love.

In the end, the park was relocated to a busy street where no one goes. The old park is fenced off as developers prepare for the next wave of gentrification. But being a good neighbor isn't about always achieving perfect outcomes. As a homeowner, Danielle remains committed to tenants' rights becoming part of the agenda in her town. That may mean fighting for a park one day and pushing against rent increases another.

Danielle has also chosen to invest in a school that has purposefully been ignored and neglected. This was not an easy decision for her and her husband. They visited the school and met the principal; they observed and asked questions. She found the staff to be dedicated and eager to receive her daughter into the classroom alongside all the refugee children. When it came to school choice, she opted in with her neighbors.

As one of the few white parents, she was quickly asked to lead the PTA. This wasn't what she had in mind. She was a writer, an introvert, and not looking for anything new to lead. But what she had in spades was a genuine affection for fellow parents and their kids. She already had established relationships with many of the mothers and understood more than most the rigors of resettlement. She knew enough about the school system to be a bridge between families and the school administration. And so in another moment of neighborliness, she agreed to serve on the PTA alongside other parents and teachers. Now she joins others in raising funds for school dances, supporting the book fair, and advocating for resources needed in the classrooms. Her investment of her time and energy in, and even the leveraging of her white privilege toward, the common good is what I call relational reparations.

We hear the word *reparations* and think of money or systems. We should; those things matter when we consider transforming unjust societies into just ones. But reparatory work also includes all the smaller ways we try to make things right in our communities with our actual neighbors. Investing our time in local schools, showing up to advocate at city council meetings, and sharing impromptu meals with our neighbors are some tangible ways we can make relational reparations. Danielle is a good neighbor: she lives in relationship with those around her and divests of her own time and energy, repurposing it for the good of her neighborhood. She is repairing the streets where she lives, making reparations one relationship at a time.

•　　　•　　　•

The kind of neighborliness we witness in Exodus is not about being nice, though we ought to always strive to be kind. What the women demonstrate is relationships with the capacity to facilitate freedom—which includes carrying the weight of reparations if necessary. The best neighbors offer not just a cup of sugar when we need it but also reparatory gestures for the deeper hurts that beset our neighborhoods.

Reparations are hard for us to talk about for many reasons. Historically, they've loomed large, like the reparations Germany made to Holocaust survivors, or that the United States government made to the Japanese American citizens incarcerated in internment camps during World War II. In both these instances, payments were made on a mass scale to make amends for systemic injustices. In the wake of apartheid in South Africa, the Truth and Reconciliation Commission (TRC) convened to embrace restorative justice and offer healing for the "rainbow nation." The commission hosted over one thousand hearings, and every Sunday night from April 1996 to June 1998 a special report on the TRC would be aired publicly so that all could participate in the reconciliation work on some level. But even the TRC was insufficient to complete the healing, the injustices of apartheid being many and complex. Even today, decades after the official end of apartheid, South Africa still struggles with residual inequalities in education, and housing and land issues remain problematic for many blacks still locked into townships.

The first time I visited South Africa, I stayed with Afrikaner friends in Stellenbosch, the lush wine country. One evening my hosts gathered their family and some friends to join us for dinner overlooking the picturesque landscape. This land had been handed down through a few generations, the father said with pride. The men, doctors and veterans, shared stories about their time serving in Angola. They spoke of their love for their country and their hopes for a future rich in reconciliation. I looked across the table, and at the portraits of their children down the hall, and felt honored to be dining with this family so steeped in the soil of this place. But I also wondered, over a glass of wine, if these friends could ever part with this land, their inheritance, in the name of justice. I thought of the pain of losing even a part of their parcel that they so cherished. Would they be willing to pay that price for reconciliation?

A few days later I rode with another friend to the township of Gugulethu, a mere twenty-two miles from the wine farms of Stellenbosch. The houses were close together, and the community was overcrowded, with people bursting out into the worn-out streets. These black families were still living in apartheid conditions, raising children in substandard housing units with little access to electricity and clean water. My friend told me that most were on waiting lists for homes the government promised to provide as reparation for their suffering under apartheid. The wait was approximately ten years. How could families live this way for another decade? How could they not hunger for their ancestral lands taken by the previous government in forced removals?

That night I was restless in South Africa. I had friends on both sides of the divide. I ached as I thought of the price of reparations, knowing who would lose land. But I wept for the children sleeping in a township again, their parents traveling hours by bus to get to and from jobs, knowing change was coming too slow for them. Reparations would be slow—and maybe not even possible. I held no illusions that they would come easily, even among people of goodwill.

Truth be told, most of us don't have the imagination for this kind of massive restorative work. We get stuck with the numbers too big to calculate, the logistics beyond our capacity.[23] How can we calculate the cost of slavery in America? How could we distribute funds to all the eligible African American descendants of enslaved people? Would it scare white people to see wealth redistributed and provoke fears about their own economic security? These are real challenges that often shut down our curiosity and imagination when it comes to large-scale reparations for systemic injustices. Like Jubilee, it's too big or too hard.

The women of Exodus demonstrate that neighborliness is where we begin to seed our imagination for true repair in our neighborhoods. When we know each other, we build relationships and lower our defenses. Our stories and struggles are shared, and neighbors know what the other has suffered. We know the sons lost—we stood at their memorials by the river. We know the hardship of the brickyards because we brought over soup when husbands were ill and gave aloe cuttings to calm irritations from the lash wounds from the incessant whippings. Neighbors know what Pharaoh's propaganda campaign omits. Neighbors cultivate compassion on the streets where they live.

God recognizes women already at work in their neighborhoods, engaging in relational reparations. The Hebrew and Egyptian women were relationally positioned for the movement of wealth, which allowed the Hebrews to leave with hope for freedom and to break the complicity of the Egyptians, utterly plundering Egypt and Pharaoh. These reparations paved the way for the Hebrews to leave like friends, not foes.

Chapter 10

DESCENDANTS OF MIRIAM
Beating Out the Rhythms of Liberation

After days spent drumming and dancing, Miriam sat down on the far side of the Reed Sea,[1] free at last. The reeds surrounding the Nile River once held her brother, keeping him safe from the speeding current. The reeds then became the meeting place of the two mothers. And now the Hebrews trampled the reeds in their exodus across a different waterway. Moses, saved by reeds and women, led the people out by way of the Sea of Reeds. Miriam knew she'd write a song about that someday.

In all her eighty years, she'd never tasted freedom. Bitterness turned to sweetness on her tongue. "Taste and see YHWH's goodness!" she exclaimed to the women encircling her. She saw the box of Patriarch Joseph's bones, exhumed and carried out of Egypt as he requested on his deathbed. It is complete now, she thought. She let out the exhale of emancipation.

What a mighty mystery! The waters rose up in translucent walls, fish dangled in upturned currents as Leviathan was effectively cut in two, and Miriam's kin walked on dry land right through the middle as if they were cutting a new covenant with YHWH.² She found herself chanting lines from her mother's lullabies—*The horse and rider will fall into the sea*—and the people echoed her back in a voluminous unison: *The horse and rider will fall into the sea!* She twirled like her younger self: *Who is like you, O Lord, among the gods?* The throngs in transit responded: *No one is like our Lord among the gods!* And when the last Hebrew heel lifted off the dried seabed, the towering barriers released like twin tsunamis, sending the Egyptian chariots crashing into the dark sea. Miriam stood by her brothers in shock, in unspoken awe.

Swirling emotions engulfed her—the sweet hit of seeing foes permanently halted from pursuit and the bitter aftertaste of her neighbors' sons and husbands dashed against the rocks at the sea's bottom. This was the moment she realized that even her deliverance wasn't a conflict-free zone. Around her, families searched for each other, making sure no one was lost or in need of care after the unconventional exit. Aaron and Moses helped organize the crowd, still buzzing with exhilaration.

Miriam, prophet, stood over the sea aching. A few widows came alongside her, sharing in her lament for the dead. "There will be empty places at their tables now," she spoke in a plaintive tone. "We know what that does to a heart." She clasped the silver pendant round her neck, a family heirloom her neighbor gave to her when they last embraced. "I will remember your son always," Miriam whispered like a prayer and a promise. The prophet, heavy with jewelry and tears, swore she heard God weeping over her shoulder. She turned to the small band of women. "Let's go down to the shore and mourn the dead, lest our own hearts calcify and become hard like Pharaoh's." And so while the Hebrews broke out their unleavened bread in the cool of that first free night, the women wept with God and the angels.³

The night crackled with campfire alchemy, an intoxicating mix of gyrating flames, smoke snaking toward the sky, the pop and hiss of golden sparks. Then the drum line sounded across the camp. Miriam pounded out a cadence unlike any other, unfettered and free. Women reached for their own drums and joined the song. The prophet started singing, harmonies building and volume increasing as her women got into formation. The prophet, yoked with wisdom, composed liberation lyrics. Over the decades, her mother's lullabies had matured into anthems of freedom inside her, now finding their fullest, truest expression. It was the longing of all the midwives and mothers together, past and present, crying out for shalom that saturated each stanza.

Miriam sang of the reversal—grown men tossed into the sea instead of infant sons. Of God's mighty arm strong to save (if a bit slow for her liking). According to some scholars, Miriam composed the earliest Hebrew freedom songs, the ones that became the liberation litany her own brother, Moses, would sing.[4]

●　　　●　　　●

I played a tambourine when I was young. It was small, made of chestnut wood and shiny with shellac. The guitar players at church would let me shake my tiny tambourine along the periphery of the circle during midweek gatherings. The tinny sound blended well enough, I suppose. My part may have been ancillary to the work of worship, but I savored every song. I fancied myself a modern Miriam swaying on the sidelines.

Years later I heard the sky crack open as Burundian drummers beat their massive drums in practiced unison with intricate rhythms and ground-shaking energy. I'd never felt anything like it—the cadence traveling through the soil, through the soles of my feet, recalibrating my heartbeat. I couldn't stand still. Dancing was instinctive. The steady, strong pounding of those drums under the golden sun unleashed what bound me, and for the duration of the drumming I stood undeniably free.

When I learned that Miriam carried a drum, not a tambourine in the modern sense, it made perfect and prophetic sense to me. The mention of a tambourine is an anachronistic mistake in translation, as much evidence in art and archeology shows that women drummed.[5] The women were trained musicians, skilled and strong with stamina to hold a rhythm all the way across the Reed Sea. They composed the victory songs and dirges, and they were at the center of the procession out of captivity and into freedom, catalyzing the community to sing. Now more than ever I want to follow in Miriam's footsteps.

In Burundi I've noticed that the Batwa women can make anything into a drum when there's reason to celebrate or gather the community. They repurpose empty plastic containers or turn washbasins upside down to find a flat surface to hammer with their calloused hands. The drums rally the women, and before long the entire village is gathered and galvanized.

These women are my favorite. They don't demand to be seen (often they crouch down low to the earth), yet they're heard across deep valleys and over green hills. Maybe they are the descendants of Miriam—it would explain my deep affinity for their playing. They drum and the community is transported to another plane, beyond hunger and discrimination, where hope lives, and we are welcomed as we dance to the rhythms meted out by the women.

What bothers me is that women can be found in the rural villages turning empty washbasins into drums and creating bass lines for their children and their community—but not in the city. Burundian drums that are hewn out of wood and hoisted on heads are reserved for men only. The male drummers parade into an open space with drums atop their ebony curls, then place them down in a large circle for their athletic performance. The women dance in fluid movements around the edges, if at all.

As guests who enjoy these performances often in the summer months, my family and I watch mesmerized. Their encore includes inviting the Westerners up front and center, allowing us to try our hand at the drumming. My son and daughter both rush up to give it a go. My son beats with flare but little sustained rhythm. My daughter, however, takes the drumsticks and begins to beat out a tight cadence using the entire span of the drum head and the sides too. She pounds with skill and absolute abandon. I watch her and imagine a young Miriam learning the freedom songs Burundi needs. My daughter can dance with grace alongside her peers, but what I want for her is to beat drums and create the conditions for liberation. It's what I want for myself— to turn in my jingly tambourine for a powerful drum.

So I'm turning in my tambourine and exchanging it for a drum that I can pound with all my might because I have freedom songs shut up in my bones. I want to break the air like a Burundian drummer and declare that Jubilee is on offer and neighborliness is making a comeback. I want to join with the tribe of women leading the liberation movement, drums in hand, because these rhythms will set us free.

◆   ◆   ◆

Miriam is the first woman in the Bible to be acknowledged as a prophet.[6] She heard from God, she spoke to the people, she moved her community on both sides of the Reed Sea. She first heard The Voice as a young girl, which assured her that her infant brother would survive the death edict and grow into a deliverer for their people. Jewish tradition says her father never got over the relinquishment of his second son, or the false hope of his daughter. But she kept hope alive.

Miriam never married. She worked with singular focus as a community organizer. The leader of drum circles, she was more than simply a music teacher or composer. Her skill set her apart as a convener and leader of women. She taught them how to listen to God's voice amid the torments of slavery. While men labored in the brickyards, Miriam wrote songs of lament for hard days and lyrics of liberation for the hoped-for days to come. Her verse and chorus in combination formed a song for singing but more importantly a theology for believing. And when she instructed the women on how to drum and sing and dance, she imparted the cadence they would need for deliverance one day. She was a voice on the wrong side of the Nile, crying out and preparing the way for YHWH to come and unleash freedom. Meanwhile she modeled patient service and sustained subversive rhythms of lament and hope in turn. She kept her people ready.

Readiness meant working the networks to ensure the relationships were in good stead. Miriam always met with women to encourage them in their deliverance work as midwives and mothers. Drum circles were times to empower her sisters with skill and to fan the flames of their hope when it waned, and she entered those meetings with the requisite seriousness. She took every opportunity to organize the women into companies of action, able to show up for one another under duress. And when the Spirit spoke, she spoke. Half the work of organizing was breathing words of life into the women so that they could continue as a counterforce of goodness.

When Miriam first hummed the melody to the Song of the Sea, I imagine her thinking about a grand reversal possible only by God's hand. The role her brothers and she herself played in the grand exit might have exceeded her expectations. The words of deliverance, of God's strong arm against Pharaoh's hard heart, poured out of her veins. She pounded out the beat as a prayer until it emerged as a song she could teach to others. According to some commentators, her song is one of the earliest theological statements from the Hebrew community.[7] Her brother may have learned the song from her, and the narrator of Exodus credits him with most of the verses. But this was the song of a prophet, a community organizer, and a public theologian. In many ways, she was the one who prepared the way for her brother to enact emancipation.

·   ·   ·

The Greater Salem Baptist Church choir welcomed a new member in 1927, a young Mahalia Jackson who had recently relocated from New Orleans to Chicago amid the Great Migration. Gospel music pumped through her veins, her true lifeblood. Her singing eventually landed her in the same room as the young Martin Luther King Jr. at the National Baptist Convention in 1956. After hearing her sing and lift the denominational gathering, he invited her to join him in Montgomery, Alabama, to sing at a fundraising rally to underwrite the cost of the bus boycott. Her songs supported the boycott and Rosa Parks, who refused to move to the back of the bus.

Mahalia continued to marry her music and activism, singing at rallies often to breathe life into the gatherings. Her songs and Martin's sermons frequently overlapped, causing a genuine friendship to develop between them. He knew all her songs, and she'd heard all his sermons.

One evening in 1963, Martin Luther King Jr. worked in a hotel room preparing a speech for the next day's event—the March for Jobs and Freedom in Washington, DC. He decided to riff on one of his tried-and-true metaphors, the bad check America had written to blacks. He felt that connected with the jobs theme of the march. The next day he and his team, including Mahalia, made their way to the steps of the Lincoln Memorial, overlooking the National Mall. She sang and then took her seat on the dais. Soon enough it was Martin's turn to offer the final exhortation for the event, so he pulled out his prepared remarks. He spoke about the bad check. But as he slowed his speech and paused, Mahalia leaned over and said, "Tell them about the dream, Martin!" Hearing her suggestion, and trusting her discernment, he said, "I have a dream . . ." The rest became the history of one of the most iconic speeches in the American canon.

He needed her in that moment. One of the most skilled orators in our nation needed the word of a woman who rightly discerned the moment. She knew what was in his repertoire. She spoke and called it out of him without apology. Thanks to their partnership, her boldness, and his ability to listen to her wisdom, we now share in their dream. When I read the Song of the Sea, I imagine Miriam and Moses with a similar partnership. She composed the lyrics, but he knew when to sing them with her. And while history often credits him with the composition, he knew the words were hers, freely shared with those emancipated from Pharaoh's empire.

• • •

Before Elizabeth celebrated her, Mary was a lowly woman betrothed to be married and to continue living in some insignificant backwater town in the grip of the merciless Roman Empire. Before the angel Gabriel visited her, she was simply Miriam of Nazareth.[8] Yes, Mary was actually Miriam. Her name was common in first-century Palestine.[9] Each young Miriam functioned as a living reminder of a prophetic woman who refused to accept death edicts, a woman who spent her energy drumming and leading people into freedom. I imagine Mary's parents, Joachim and Anne, wanted her to beat her drum like her namesake once did and push against pharaonic injustice in whatever small way she could.[10] And this is precisely what God chose her to do.

In the company of her cousin Elizabeth, Mary sang a song of revolutionary reversal. The Magnificat, as it is traditionally known, extols the Mighty One who performs salvific deeds with his arm on behalf of the oppressed of the world. The echo of Miriam's song of long ago can be heard, both women praising the God who dethrones rulers, casting their militaries into the depths in favor of the lowly ones. This God, Mary sings, lifts the humble and fills the hungry with good things. She sensed early on that Elizabeth wouldn't be the only one to call her blessed in the generations to come. God continued the grand reversal by lifting Miriam from lowly Nazarene girl to Mother of God.

Mary imagined that her baby would continue the upending of empires that God began back in Egypt. A deliverer from the lineage of King David, her boy would bring down the powerful overlords and elevate the downtrodden of the land. Her son would keep faith with the God who feeds the hungry, distributes justice, and frees the captive. Born in a stable on the outskirts of Bethlehem, he would one day ascend to the Father's right hand. Like his mother, he would reveal that good things come from Nazareth, turning popular expectations on their head.

Throughout her life, Mary pondered the God who overshadowed her. She hummed her magnificent song of overturned expectations as her son learned Torah and took on the mantle of rabbi in Galilee. She sang it through tears to console herself as he hung on a cross at Golgotha, when she didn't understand what her world was coming to anymore. And on Easter Sunday—how full and glorious the song must have sounded then! Maybe by then her friends knew the chorus, and the women sang with her as the resurrection reversed death itself.

I listen to Mary hum as I read the stories about her Jesus. I witness her bravery to sing of revolution under the thumb of the Roman Empire. She was brave to believe God's announcement to her, holding fast to the song in the face of years of conflicting messages and even crucifixion. She let the song grow into an anthem as her son grew into the Messiah. That liberation anthem called out the best in her, giving her words to sing, full voiced, even when all evidence proclaimed something quite contrary. She never stopped believing in God's grand reversal.

We can join Mother Mary, and Mary Magdalene too, for that matter, whom Jesus called by her Hebrew name on Easter Sunday: Miriam. We can sing of revolutionary reversals in which the vulnerable will lead viable lives, the meek will inherit the land, where rulers will be dethroned and chariots tossed into the sea. This is our anthem as we confront new pharaohs and labor for fresh liberation on our horizon.

◆　　　◆　　　◆

"Sí, se puede!" she cried out. "Sí, se puede!"[11] the farm workers echoed back with vigor. It was Dolores Huerta, a Mexican American activist and labor leader, who created this rallying cry. In 1972, her colleague Cesar Chavez was on a hunger strike (what he saw as a fast in accordance with his Catholic tradition) in Arizona that would last twenty-five days. This was his response to the recent passage of anti-boycott legislation passed in the state against farmers. Dolores's response was to speak out and lead farmers in vocal support of Chavez while exposing the injustice of the law that tried to silence the migrant work force.

Dolores was born in New Mexico in 1930, at the beginning of the Great Depression. Her mother, Alicia, raised her in the agricultural landscape of Stockton, California. Alicia, an industrious woman, owned a restaurant and a modest hotel and ran them with her trademark kindness. She welcomed low-income guests and, when times were desperate, even allowed farmers to stay for free when they could not afford other accommodations. Dolores grew in the shadow of her mother, watching her hospitality at work in the community. She, like a young Miriam, was inspired by her mother's example.

As Dolores grew alongside the fields in California, she became deeply aware of the struggle of the migrant workers who were her neighbors. She knew their dismal living conditions—shanties without heat or running water, and little food to feed their families. As the workers moved, following the various harvests, that life offered no stability for the parents but even less for children who often went without education. Dolores began her career as a teacher but decided her energy could be better spent elsewhere. "I couldn't tolerate seeing kids come to class hungry and needing shoes. I thought

I could do more by organizing farm workers than by trying to teach their hungry children."[12] And so she started her life's work as an organizer.

Armed with a strong intellect, rhetorical verve, and an abundance of compassion for farm workers, she launched several initiatives to help improve the working conditions of migrant workers. She is best known for her collaboration with Cesar Chavez, another local organizer. Together they cofounded the association that became the United Farm Workers (UFW). While their relationship was fiery from the start, they managed to advocate in new ways for the workers in the California fields. They led a strike against grape growers, bringing national attention to the plight of the field workers through a grape boycott. Eventually the growers came to the bargaining table, and it was Dolores who negotiated the first workers' contract for improved pay and working conditions. The strength of her and Cesar's actions included fomenting solidarity between Chicano and other migrant communities, like the Filipino workers. Banding together improved conditions for all the workers, though it was a constant struggle against the resources of agribusiness. She organized and rallied for decades.

There were more strikes, rallies, and fasts. Dolores held to her nonviolent values, clinging to Our Lady of Guadalupe, known as a patron saint of liberation for Mexican American women. But she was arrested twenty-two times. She was beaten and hospitalized. Her story has even been censored in public schools.[13] Many know her as a troublemaker. I'm sure that not everyone loved Miriam either, strident organizer and a relentless voice rallying the labor force. But both women knew in their bones that liberation was possible: *sí, se puede, hermanas, sí, se puede.*

•　　•　　•

The protests ignited by the deaths of Michael Brown in Ferguson and Eric Garner in New York stirred my conscience; the Black Lives Matter movement spoke to what I feared for my own black son. One voice sounded out above all others, catching my attention with more than her colorful hijab. Linda Sarsour, a Palestinian American born, raised, and proudly residing in Brooklyn, marched alongside black mothers, clergywomen, and the entire mixed crowd. She stood erect and walked with purpose, confidence radiating from her countenance. She reminded me of someone I could not place, but Linda was both mesmerizing and familiar.

Linda helped lead a march from New York to Washington, DC, in 2015 to honor Eric Garner and other black men killed by police. The next year she helped raise over $100,000 to rebuild black churches that were burned across the South in the wake of the massacre at Emanuel African Methodist Episcopal Church in Charleston. The following year she stood in the bitter cold of Standing Rock with the Indigenous communities gathered there to say in unison, "Water is life." In 2017, a Jewish cemetery in St. Louis was subjected to anti-Semitic acts of vandalism. Linda rallied the Muslim community to raise funds to restore the gravesites and to repair other damage in an act of solidarity with the Jewish community. She appealed to people with a voice that commanded attention, a modern siren of justice. Her words were strong, strident, and unflinching. In every instance she insisted that our communities hold these issues in common; when any are oppressed, we all are in peril.

She spoke up everywhere she was invited, and places she wasn't, demanding justice for all marginalized people. She addressed her own Muslim community, asking them, "What are you doing for Black Lives Matter now—both inside and outside the Muslim community?" You could feel her pushing them to see that these injustices, and the necessary responses, are not corralled within communities but are shared by all of us. She challenged the packed auditorium: "What are you willing to do? Are you prepared?" In her cry meant to activate them, I recognized the voice. It was the voice of Miriam imploring her women to be ready. When Linda told her Muslim brothers and sisters that she planned to be "perpetually outraged" in the face of this current pharaoh, I imagined Miriam saying similar words to her women as they tended their drums. "Pharaoh does not rest, and neither can we."

The day after the inauguration of the forty-fifth president, women took to the streets across the United States and all seven continents to showcase our concerns for the new administration to see. Linda was one of the codirectors of the Women's March, quite possibly the largest single-day protest ever recorded. She organized across different groups and concerns and worked alongside a variety of women to fill the streets. While Linda marched with her sisters in Washington, DC, I took my first steps of protest in Phoenix, following her lead.

I learned how to pray with my feet that day, walking with so many other women through our downtown streets and past our statehouse. I walked in lockstep with women who represented their communities—some wearing hijabs, others crocheted pink caps, some carrying placards with the image of a strong Latina woman, and others draped in Indigenous jewelry. This coming together of women felt holy. For the first time in many months, I witnessed hope rising. This is the work of women like Linda, like Dolores, and like Miriam, who convene and mobilize us toward action. The fruit of their labor breaks our isolation and moves us forward together to shape new futures.

•   •   •

We are all Miriam's descendants with work to do, songs to sing, and liberation to practice until every pharaoh is dethroned and every captive set free. Women are not the soft side of church work. We aren't meant to educate only women and children. We are not serving well only when we are supporting the men in leadership. We are called to be Exodus strong and to work alongside men to set people on both sides of the Nile free from slavery, complicity, and all manner of injustice. Liberation work is part of our Exodus mandate.

The women in the Exodus narrative demonstrate the valuable and necessary energy of women of faith at work in the world. They see in a certain way that is instructive for us. Shiphrah and Puah saw no difference in gender when they delivered children; their sight was rooted in their fear of God. Pharaoh saw in order to differentiate and divide, but the midwives saw with deeper discernment—they saw life. Jochebed saw the creation goodness in her son, and saw a possible ally in the woman across the river. Bithiah saw the Hebrew baby and the chance to rescue him from death by her father's edict. The seven sisters of Midian saw the Egyptian who saved them from the shepherds, and they introduced him to their father. In the darkness Zipporah saw that Moses was under threat and moved swiftly to deliver him from death. Without these women, who saw clearly and acted accordingly, Moses would not have survived Egypt or Midian.

Miriam saw the future of her baby brother before he was even born. She watched her mother place him in the reeds and stepped in when Bithiah needed her help. She grew into a woman who saw the need for a liberation theology and songs to move that message across the community. And she saw what her father never lived to see: her prophecy come true as Moses took the Hebrews across the Reed Sea into freedom. Miriam saw with eyes of faith, led her people with that vision, and served alongside her brothers to see liberation realized.

These women had eyes that discerned but didn't discriminate. They had eyes that saw the problems and imagined solutions. Their eyes saw opportunities and propelled them to wade into dangerous waters to save others. Their eyes saw goodness and pain and the possibility of liberation. Our sight must be shaped by our fear of God, not fixated on numbers and delusions of greatness. We need fresh eyes to see how we can create the conditions for liberation to confront the pharaonic forces of our day.

The way the Exodus women looked out onto their landscape shaped how they behaved in their world. They obeyed their creation call to be fruitful and multiply and usher in shalom. Under duress, they did this with acts of defiance, risk, and rescue. Amid danger, the young still stepped forward to lead, women mothered, and a Nile network operated in solidarity across the river. They practiced the sacraments and neighborly reparations and all manner of community organizing to make it out of Egypt. We need nothing less today.

And the men needed the women to play their part in the labor of liberation. Martin Luther King Jr. needed Mahalia Jackson, Oskar Schindler needed Emilie Schindler, and Moses needed his sister, Miriam. In each of these instances, freedom came when men and women worked toward emancipation in tandem. It took the twelve sons of Israel and the twelve women of Exodus to cross over the Reed Sea. And it remains true today that liberation can be birthed only when men and women collaborate, being fruitful and multiplying together for the sake of freedom for all. Then and now, liberation takes all of us.

The women of Exodus remain strong archetypes for us as we enter into the liberative work of our own era. They help us crack open our imaginations for the long walk of freedom that remains ahead.

We are Miriam's descendants. So it's time we compose more freedom songs and dedicate more time to drum circles. It's time we move in stride together to lead our communities out of bondage, out of scarcity, and out of injustice.

It is our turn to carry Miriam's drum.

Study Questions

Paige and Sean Whiting

INTRODUCTION

1. What does your faith community explicitly say about the role of women in the church? Does the implicit reality match what is said, or is it different?

2. The idea of liberation and its close connection with social justice have sometimes been criticized as peripheral to the gospel message, secondary to salvation and eternal life. How do you view social justice? Are you passionately committed to it, uncomfortable with it, or somewhere in between?

3. Readers of biblical stories usually identify with the underdogs or the ones on whom the narrator focuses, but if we come from a place of privilege, it might be more accurate to read the story from the point of view of the powerful. With whom do you naturally and realistically identify in the Exodus story?

4. As you begin, take some time to read Exodus 1–3 and 15. This will help remind you of the Exodus story and specifically the women on whom we will focus.

CHAPTER 1. TWELVE MEN, TWELVE WOMEN

1. Reflect on your experience of being overlooked or dismissed because of gender, race, or other identities. Can you empathize with the women of Exodus?

2. How would you define and identify "shalom"? What are its key characteristics, and who participates in shalom? What is the difference between shalom and "utopia"?

3. The author frequently mentions "liberation" and "liberation work" on a communal level. What is meant by "liberation"? Have you ever participated in liberation work for your neighborhood or wider community?

4. Do you agree that female contributions in history tend to be overlooked or dismissed in the telling of stories, from Exodus to NASA? How would stories be different if women told them?

5. "When all women are invited into the full work of the church—with their heart, mind, soul, and strength—imagine what strongholds could be torn down" (p. 20). In what areas are women welcomed or not welcomed in your church or faith community? If women are not welcomed in some areas, is this explicit or implicit? How would your desire for participation in the "full work" of the church or faith community be received?

CHAPTER 2. SHIPHRAH AND PUAH: FREEDOM THROUGH DISOBEDIENCE

1. Have you ever been asked to believe something or do something that you knew was not the intention or heart of God?

How did you respond? How did you *want* to respond? What inspiration can you receive from the Hebrew midwives, Shiphrah and Puah?

2. Who would you classify as the "Hebrews" of today in our world? Do you know anyone in the group of people you just identified?

3. Looking back on the Hebrew midwives of history and Rosa Parks of yesteryear, we admire their courage and vision for social justice, bringing life in the face of death. Are justice causes of our day harder to identify and/or hard to join?

4. "Fearing God requires acute discernment, mastery of wits, and some subversive strength" (pp. 33-34). What does this sentence mean to you? How does one's faith in God lead to defiance and even the occasional lie for a greater good?

5. What are the current events or issues that might move you to action for the sake of shalom in your neighborhood? Is defiance, such as the Hebrew midwives displayed, or civil disobedience, such as Rosa Parks exhibited, required for shalom to be realized in your larger community? Are you willing to risk status, comfort, and acceptance for those who are part of this collective shalom? Have you ever made space in your life for those who are different from you?

6. The author shares about current Pharaohs of our land. In this chapter, do you identify more with the Hebrews or the Egyptians? In our modern world, do you normally identify with those in power or those with little or no power?

CHAPTER 3. JOCHEBED: FREEDOM THROUGH RELINQUISHMENT

1. The author uses "sanctified imagination" (p. 8) to take literary license to help us understand the political and personal environment in Egypt for Hebrew mothers. Are you comfortable with this imaginative thinking that expounds the sacred text? Why or why not?

2. This chapter speaks of no less than four women, in addition to Jochebed, who have played a subversive and risk-filled role to defy unjust laws and policies in their time (Nurse Lydia, Mama Rose, Emelie Schindler, and Patricia Nombuyiselo Noah). What do these women hold in common despite their vastly different lives and situations? What do their environments hold in common?

3. Relinquishment is a subtheme of the work of freedom. Why is the act of relinquishment almost always required in bringing liberation and freedom? What must often be given up individually for the community to prosper? What have you relinquished in your life for the greater good? What could you relinquish in future liberation work?

4. The author speaks of Egyptian injustice becoming widespread when Pharaoh issued edicts for all the citizenry. Complicity through indifference or blind following of unjust laws ensued. Are there any laws of your current land that make you complicit to injustice if you choose to look away indifferently or support the laws willingly?

5. Freedom and justice in Exodus took many, many years to achieve. Are you working for the liberation of someone, or

more than one person, now and feeling like it will never come? How do you maintain the will to keep persevering?

CHAPTER 4. BITHIAH: FREEDOM THROUGH LEVERAGED PRIVILEGE

1. The author states that you (the reader) and she are "like Bithiah," that the ease and benefit of the way of life we were born into can begin to cause discomfort as we notice the hurting world around us. Do you agree that your life is like Bithiah's? Why or why not?

2. Once Bithiah saw the truth, "there were decisions to be made" (p. 64). What kinds of decisions did Bithiah need to wrestle with even before drawing the baby Moses out of the Nile River?

3. The author portrays Sarah in a negative light for her treatment of Hagar. Is this a fair portrayal? Have you ever heard the story of Sarah and Abraham from the perspective of Hagar? How does this perspective enrich the story?

4. "Ask Allah to protect him, and I will implore Jesus to intervene" (p. 69). Have you ever aligned yourself or been in some kind of partnership or solidarity with someone of another faith? How have you or how would you participate in a cross-faith friendship or project for either personal or social reasons?

5. What is meant by "taking a personal inventory of your privilege" (p. 74)? Why is this necessary in liberation work and in building solidarity with fellow freedom workers? What is your most privileged power in society? Why?

6. "Most effective strategies for liberation will be initiated by those with less power" (p. 75). Why does the author think those with less power have better strategies for helping others gain freedom? What does this sentence mean to you? Why might those without power have insight that others who have power might not?

CHAPTER 5. MIRIAM: FREEDOM THROUGH YOUTHFUL ZEAL

1. This chapter imagines the inner conflict Bithiah has as she begins to see the world from the perspective of the outsiders, the ones without any voice or power in her society. What does Bithiah do, and not do, to educate herself about a perspective that she is unfamiliar with?

2. Since the voice and perspective of the oppressed so often go unnoticed, this chapter dwells at length on stories of people who are underneath the powerful in society (government, the rich, the powerful), such as Tahany. Are you comfortable hearing such stories? Why or why not?

3. The author gives many examples of young leaders giving voice to societal problems in new ways. What is it about young people that makes them potential workers for freedom and liberation?

4. "Emma [González] spoke in the way I imagine Miriam spoke that day at the river's edge, cheeks wet with tears but voice strong with conviction" (p. 84). What specific problem in your neighborhood or community has broken your heart? Could this be the area into which you are being called to de-

vote energy and effort for liberation work? In what ways have your cheeks been wet with tears but your voice strong with conviction?

CHAPTER 6. MOTHERS ALL: FREEDOM
THROUGH MOTHERING

1. Doing the often subversive work of justice, promoting life in the face of death, takes courage and even cunning. What kind of relationship do you think Bithiah and Jochebed forged during their daring rescue of Moses? Was it affectionate? Simply strategic? What kind of relationships do you hope to have with others working alongside you in the sometimes grueling work of liberation?

2. "Mothering opened me to peacemaking in a different way. It made me recognize the interconnection and need for solidarity in societies that are often harsh on those with darker skin, those who are foreign-born, or those who speak with accents" (p. 103). When you think of your community, how does this sentence resonate? Who is the "other" in your neighborhood?

3. The author shares candidly about her deeply emotional response and fear stemming from the murder of Trayvon Martin. When has your heart broken because of injustice? What were the circumstances? What was your response? How would you respond now?

4. Expanding the role and skills of motherhood to a larger community can be significant in peacemaking work of all kinds. What gifts and mothering abilities do you see in your commu-

nity that could be mobilized for the justice work that is needed? What gifts or experiences will you pass down to your own children and community?

5. "Mothering is not exclusive to women who give birth but, rather, a hallmark of women who sponsor life" (p. 111). As you read and imagine the women of Exodus, how has your view of motherhood or womanhood been influenced?

CHAPTER 7. THE SEVEN SISTERS OF MIDIAN: FREEDOM THROUGH SOLIDARITY

1. What is your initial response to the author's reference to the Qur'an? Does this enhance or distract from your exploration of the biblical text and the women of Exodus? Why?

2. As the author imagines the working life of the sisters of Midian, how does your own work life resonate with theirs? How does it not resonate? How has patriarchy changed or not changed from their time to now?

3. Is there anyone you know who has been particularly affected by patriarchy? Does this person or people have anyone who is standing up for them? Why or why not?

4. "Sisterhood opens the door to reciprocal transformation whereby we all become more human and more free together" (p. 124). When have you most experienced solidarity with sisters or others for a just cause? How did that group initially form, and what held it together in trying times?

5. How are identity and freedom connected? What made Moses identify as Hebrew despite knowing only Egyptian cul-

ture? What made the author explore and adopt a long-forgotten Latina heritage?

6. When a hyena attacks a doe, the rest of the herd knows they could defend her if they work together, yet each hesitates, fearing that the others won't join in the defense. Can you relate to the doe being attacked, helpless unless the herd comes to the defense? Can you identify with the hesitating doe? Or both?

7. Reread the author's main thesis about women's work for justice (p. 129):

> Sisterhood moves toward solidarity when we are willing to listen deeply to the stories of our sisters who've been hurt by injustice—even injustice we've benefited from in some way. Our hearing and their healing are interconnected. We begin to see ways we've participated in the injustice, then we repent and unlearn our inherited ways. We commit to walk with our sisters, putting down our swords and spears and refashioning them into ploughs and pruning hooks so that we can work the fields together, then gather and feast. The shared work of solidarity is an embodiment of shalom.

What influences in your life, if any, have carried this theme or a similar one? Are these ideas completely new, or do they articulate something you've always known or practiced?

CHAPTER 8. ZIPPORAH: FREEDOM THROUGH SACRAMENT

1. Sacraments are understood and practiced differently across denominations and streams of Christian community.

What understanding and experiences do you bring to this chapter regarding sacraments of the church? Have you ever found yourself in a position that resonates with the author about the longing to share a "sacramental moment" together with other believers in Christ (p. 137)?

2. Read Exodus 4:18-25, in which Zipporah saves Moses from God's intention to kill him. How does this wild element of the Exodus story sit with you? Do you remember reading this part of the passage before? Was Zipporah really so essential to ensuring the deliverance of the Hebrews (pp. 143-44) at this foundational moment of the Jewish people?

3. "A salvation oracle is meant to break the power of nightmares by reminding us that all is well" (p. 146). From what night terrors or other false beliefs have you been freed by someone speaking salvation oracles over you? What were the words spoken that brought a sense of freedom?

4. How does the practice of sacrament contribute to liberation work (pp. 146-47)? Has your understanding of sacrament changed as you read through this chapter? How do you understand a sacramental way of living?

CHAPTER 9. THE NILE NETWORK: FREEDOM THROUGH NEIGHBORLINESS

1. "Extreme duress pushed the Hebrew and Egyptian daughters to embody a solidarity that would erode the empire" (p. 149). In preparing for true solidarity, the kind that is forged through difficulty, what practices can be put into place for you to be ready to engage in your community for liberation?

2. The author imagines Hebrew women and Egyptian women crossing paths often in common public spaces. Do you have much daily contact with people who are different from you in skin color, economic status, educational level, nationality, or other identities? With whom do you rub shoulders in everyday life, and with whom might you one day be unified against imperial demands? How are neighborliness and freedom connected?

3. In what ways are you a beneficiary of imperial policies and expectations (political and/or cultural)? How might this make you "complicit" (pp. 151–52)? How can you move from beneficiary to advocate for those who aren't benefiting in the same way as you?

4. In this chapter we learn about Dalia, a European woman who learned she was living in the house of an Arab family that was forced to flee because of Israeli government demands. What was it about Dalia that helped her respond with compassion when she realized the truth about her house and sought to make reparations?

5. The author suggests that in the Hebrews leaving Egypt with a recompense of jewelry and other goods, "all are set free" (p. 158), Hebrew and Egyptian alike. How is it that the Egyptians would be "freed" by the Hebrew "plundering"?

6. What are your thoughts on the idea of reparations? How are injustice and reparations intertwined? Are there other biblical examples of reparations being given (given back) for previous injustice? If you come from a place of privilege, how can you play a role in relational reparations such Danielle does in her ethnically diverse neighborhood on the outskirts of Portland?

CHAPTER 10. DESCENDANTS OF MIRIAM: BEATING OUT
THE RHYTHMS OF LIBERATION

1. Take some time now to reread Exodus 1–3 and 15. Do you read this story differently than when you started this book? If so, in what ways?

2. The author describes the Hebrew women, not celebrating, but lamenting at the Sea of Reeds over the dead of Egypt (p. 169). How do you respond to this description? Would you feel more sorrow or triumph?

3. How has your comfort level with ideas of liberation or stories of social justice grown or changed as you've read this book? Why did you first start reading this book? Are you surprised, relieved, inspired, or unsure about where it has taken you?

4. Mahalia Jackson, Dolores Huerta, and Linda Sarsour are offered as modern-day Miriams in this chapter. Can you think of additional public figures or even personal ones in your life that have inspired you? In what ways have public figures or private individuals known to you made you uncomfortable with their actions on behalf of marginalized or overlooked people?

5. Is there a certain issue or action that has been a drumbeat on your heart as you have read these stories of freedom from Egypt and have taken them to our current world? What are the first steps you might take to begin (or continue) the liberation work in your community? Do you have a person or several people in mind you might recruit or join to be part of your own Nile network or sisters in solidarity for shalom?

Acknowledgments

Writing a book requires a pen and a pruning hook, solitary time and communal input. I am indebted to my community, those who made this work stronger with their honest and spirited engagement.

First I must thank Annie Rim, the midwife for this book. The first to read each chapter and offer comments, the one who engaged in months upon months of conversation about big ideas and small details, and who endured all my emotions throughout the publication process. Her companionship ensured that the writing process was not lonely but full of deep dialogue and levity.

I owe a debt of gratitude to the two women who initially saw the potential in this project centered on the women of Exodus. The first time I preached about the liberation work of women, Rachelle Gardner rushed toward me and said, "This is your next book!" (Always trust your literary agent!) Shortly after, Lil Copan shared her enthusiasm and acquired the book. (Always trust the sharpest editor in the business!)

D. L. Mayfield and Amy Peterson offered copious and candid editorial notes, combing through my entire manuscript. They tightened the structure, strengthened arguments, corrected grammar, challenged my assumptions, and gave me the courage to write with more vulnerability. Their editorial work was invaluable; each note made me feel deeply seen and loved.

My writing community includes the loyal and literary women I affectionately call "the laureates." Thank you to Amy Peterson, Christiana Peterson, D. L. Mayfield, Jessica Goudeau, and Stina Kielsmeier-Cook for sharing the writing life with me. We've enjoyed a golden season, each bringing a book to publication. We've embodied our informal mantra: Write like a mother!

I am deeply grateful for other conversation partners who made the writing season sweeter. Thanks to Idelette McVicker, Sarah Bessey, Kaitlin Curtice, Nicole York, and Sherry Naron for sharing the journey, day in and day out. Their robust friendship buoyed me from Burundi to Arizona. I am thankful for the continued support of Laura Shook and the contributions offered by Lynne Hybels and Elie Pritz. No writing project is a singular effort. In my case, it took a village of strong women!

I appreciate the generous contribution of Sean and Paige Whiting, who read, digested, and dialogued through the ideas in this book and created a robust discussion guide to facilitate many more conversations about women, liberation, and justice in our communities.

I am also thankful for books rich with substantive footnotes, and for coffee shops (Starbucks in Surprise, Arizona, and Café Gourmand in Bujumbura, Burundi) that keep me caffeinated.

And finally, thank you to Claude Nikondeha. In the most

practical ways, he made my writing life possible with his constant support. He believed in my work long before I did. At every twist and every turn, he cheers me on, encourages my ambition, and pushes me to imagine more. A large part of my freedom comes from our partnership.

Notes

CHAPTER 1

1. Genesis 47:1–12.

2. Exodus 1:7, emphasis mine.

3. U. Cassuto points to this as "seven expressions for increase" and "a number indicative of perfection." Cassuto, *A Commentary on the Book of Exodus* (Jerusalem: The Hebrew University Magnes Press, 1967), 9.

4. Lisa Sharon Harper, *The Very Good Gospel: How Everything Wrong Can Be Made Right* (Colorado Springs: WaterBrook, 2016), 29–30. I'm indebted to Harper for her theologically rich and accessible explanation of dominion in the creation context. Her entire chapter "A Glimpse of Shalom" is a brilliant description of the creation mandate.

5. Harper, *The Very Good Gospel*, 84. The entire chapter "Shalom Between Genders" is recommended reading.

6. Exodus 1:1.

7. The Hebrew title of the book of Exodus is *Sefer Sh'mot*, meaning "The Book: Names" or "The Book of Names." This is taken from the first words of the book.

8. Cassuto, *Commentary on Exodus*, 7.

9. An *igitenge* (plural *ibitenge*) is the African fabric the women wear around their waist like a skirt, sometimes over their shoulders like a wrap. Often they will tie it like a cape around their neck to shield the baby on their back from the harsh sunlight. For rural Burundian women, it is often the

most costly and treasured item they own, something given at their wedding and worn until it is threadbare.

10. The vote established not only new leaders, including the women, but also a nimbler leadership structure for the community, which reduced the traditional twelve positions to five.

11. For further conversation on what women contribute to church and local communities worldwide, I recommend both *Half the Sky: Turning Oppression into Opportunity for Women Worldwide* by Nicholas D. Kristof and Sheryl Wu-Dunn (New York: Vintage, 2010) and *Half the Church: Recapturing God's Global Vision for Women* by Carolyn Custis James (Grand Rapids: Zondervan, 2011).

12. Luke 8:1–3.

13. Renita J. Weems, *Just A Sister Away: A Womanist Vision of Women's Relationships in the Bible* (San Diego: LuraMedia, 1988), 86.

14. Weems, *Just A Sister Away*, 86.

15. Exodus 1:8.

16. Walter Brueggemann, "The Book of Exodus," in *The New Interpreter's Bible: A Commentary in Twelve Volumes*, vol. 1 (Nashville: Abingdon, 1994), 694.

17. Exodus 1:9.

18. Cassuto, *Commentary on Exodus*, 10.

19. Exodus 1:12.

20. Another seven words are used in Exodus 1:13–14—not words of fruitfulness like in Exodus 1:7, but seven words derived from the Hebrew stem meaning "rigor" and "serve, service, work": "So the Egyptians made the children of Israel *work* with *rigor* and made their lives bitter with hard *service*, in mortar and brick, and in all kinds of *work* in the field, in addition to all their *work*, wherein they made them *serve* with *rigor*" (Cassuto's translation). The Hebrews have moved from shalom to slavery, and we can hear it in the text itself. Cassuto, *Commentary on Exodus*, 12.

21. *Hidden Figures* debuted in movie theaters in 2016 and is based on the nonfiction book by Margot Lee Shetterly, *Hidden Figures: The American Dream and the Untold Story of the Black Women Who Helped Win the Space Race* (New York: William Morrow, 2016).

22. I'm grateful for Carol Meyers, who noticed the twelve women as "rhetorical counterparts to the twelve tribes." Carol Meyers, *Exodus* (Cambridge: Cambridge University Press, 2005), 37.

CHAPTER 2

1. Wilda C. Gafney, *Womanist Midrash: A Reintroduction to the Women of the Torah and the Throne* (Louisville: Westminster John Knox, 2017), 89.

2. Exodus 1:15–16, my paraphrase.

3. See Exodus 1:7 and page 10.

4. See *Mirror to the Church: Resurrecting Faith after Genocide in Rwanda* by Emmanuel Katongole with Jonathan Wilson-Hartgrove (Grand Rapids: Zondervan, 2009) for an insightful exploration of identity, tribalism, and violence in Rwanda and beyond.

5. U. Cassuto points out that the keyword in Exodus 1:15-21 is *midwife*, and it occurs seven times. As before with the seven mentions of strength in Exodus 1:7 and hard work in Exodus 1:14-16, we are meant to see the emphases of the narrative. The midwives are the focus of this interaction with the Egyptian ruler. U. Cassuto, *A Commentary on the Book of Exodus* (Jerusalem: The Hebrew University Magnes Press, 1967), 15.

6. Cassuto, *Commentary on the Book of Exodus*, 13.

7. Carol Meyers offers a helpful excursus on midwives and wet nurses in *Exodus* (Cambridge: Cambridge University Press, 2005), 40-41.

8. Avivah Gottlieb Zornberg, *The Particulars of Rapture: Reflections on Exodus* (New York: Schocken Books, 2001), 23. Zornberg writes, "This midwives' disobedience is described with an idiom that has never before appeared in the Torah in just this form: 'they feared God.' . . . [The midwives] enact the fear of God: they 'do' it."

9. We are not told directly by the narrator why boys were the target of Pharaoh's campaign. Some commentators mention how this seems to cut the labor force and therefore is a self-defeating measure on his behalf (see, e.g., Walter Brueggemann, "The Book of Exodus," in *The New Interpreter's Bible: A Commentary in Twelve Volumes*, vol. 1 [Nashville: Abingdon, 1994], 694). Others call it population control—maybe an effort to curb the rapid increase of the Israelites (see, e.g., Meyers, *Exodus*, 36). But I tend to agree with Peter Enns that Pharaoh saw the boys as a potential military threat (*Exodus: The NIV Application Commentary* [Grand Rapids: Zondervan, 2000], 44). As we see in previous verses, he was concerned that the sons of Goshen would rise up in armed revolt with invading foreign powers. Pharaoh viewed the boys as a future security risk, and he wanted to nip the threat in the bud—or birth canal, as the case is here.

10. Nahum Sarna, *Exploring Exodus: The Origins of Biblical Israel* (New York: Schocken Books, 1996), 25.

11. Exodus 1:18.

12. Exodus 1:19.

13. Proverbs 14:26-27.

14. Dr. Rob Stegmann, Pauline scholar, says Romans 13 is not an endorsement of government authority. Paul and his readers were embedded in a concrete culture that shaped these conversations. How we interpret the passage might say more about which side of the power differential *we* stand on. Personal interview, February 2, 2018.

15. Brueggemann, "The Book of Exodus," 696.

16. Sarna, *Exploring Exodus*, 18.

17. Exodus 1:12.

18. Exodus 1:22.

19. Nahum Sarna comments so clearly on this point: "Thwarted once again in his evil designs, the pharaoh now enlists 'all his people,' the entire apparatus of the state, in a national effort to systemically annihilate the people of Israel." Sarna, *Exploring Exodus*, 26.

20. Gafney, *Womanist Midrash*, 91.

21. Psalms 22:9; 71:6, 21.

22. L. Juliana M. Claassens, *Mourner, Mother, Midwife: Reimagining God's Delivering Presence in the Old Testament* (Louisville: Westminster John Knox, 2012), 78.

CHAPTER 3

1. Wilda C. Gafney mentions the turning fortunes of Jochebed's family during their tenure in Egypt. She makes a connection to the Jews who lived in Europe before the Holocaust, noting the similarities as both communities watched their world change within their lifetime. Gafney, *Womanist Midrash: A Reintroduction to the Women of the Torah and the Throne* (Louisville: Westminster John Knox, 2017), 92.

2. Numbers 26:59 NRSV: "The name of Amram's wife was Jochebed daughter of Levi, who was born to Levi in Egypt . . ." (cf. Exod. 6:16-20). Some translations of this verse, such as the New International Version and the New Living Translation, change "daughter" to "descendant" and say Jochebed was born "to the Levites." But "according to the MT [Masoretic Text], SP [Samaritan Pentateuch], and dominant Targumim, Jochebed is the daughter of the patriarch himself, literally *bat Levi*, and not just a woman among his descendants." Gafney, *Womanist Midrash*, 92.

3. Exodus 2:2.

4. The Hebrew word used in Exodus 2:2 is *tov*, echoing the word used in Genesis 1:31. As Walter Brueggemann points out, "The birth [of Moses] is a new act of creation, an act of new creation. The world begins here again, precisely out of the chaos that 'the new king' had decreed." Brueggemann, "The Book of Exodus," in *The New Interpreter's Bible: A Commentary in Twelve Volumes*, vol. 1 (Nashville: Abingdon, 1994), 699.

5. Exodus 6:20 and also Numbers 26:59, which names her husband and all three children.

6. Walter Brueggemann calls this birth, and those like it, "an act of raw danger." Brueggemann, "The Book of Exodus," 699.

7. For more on Kallie Wood and her story, see www.convergingpathways.ca.

8. The United States also took children from unwed mothers in what is called the Baby Scoop Era. For more on this history, refer to *The Child Catchers: Rescuing, Trafficking, and the New Gospel of Adoption* by Kathryn Joyce (New York: PublicAffairs, 2013).

9. For more about the effects of trauma on individuals and communities and how they are transmitted through the generations, I recommend *Trauma Trails: Recreating Song Lines — The Transgenerational Effects of Trauma in Indigenous Australia* by Judy Atkinson (North Melbourne: Spinifex, 2002).

10. In Ecclesiastes 11:1, "casting bread on the water" might be a reference to an Egyptian agrarian practice of casting forth grain seed during the annual flooding of the Nile; it appears that you are throwing the seed on the water, but it will seep into the fertile soil. Other commentators say it might refer to the way rice is planted in marshlands. Still others say this verse is about hospitality offered to many people, even or especially those who have no prospects of returning the favor. You never know where generosity might sprout in the future . . . This echoes the parable Jesus told in Luke 14:15–23. It turns out that, when the poor or the traumatized cannot repay, God offers an eternal reciprocity to those who are generous with their hospitality. See my book *Adopted: The Sacrament of Belonging in a Fractured World* (Grand Rapids: Eerdmans, 2017), 76–77.

11. The Holocaust was the final solution that shook the modern world. I can think of other genocides and atrocities across Africa, apartheid, the Nakba, the transatlantic slave trade, Jim Crow laws, and the "New Jim Crow" (the war on drugs that leads to the mass incarceration of black people) . . . to name just some of the death edicts imagined and implemented by modern-day pharaohs.

12. See chapter 6, note 7.

13. Matthew 13:33. The parable is told again in Luke 13:20–21.

14. According to Amy-Jill Levine, *enkrypto* (and its cognate *krypto*) "refers not only to something that is hidden, but to something that should or must be uncovered . . . what is hidden must be made manifest." The sense is that when you hide something, it is only a matter of time before the results are revealed. Amy-Jill Levine, *Short Stories by Jesus: The Enigmatic Parables of a Controversial Rabbi* (San Francisco: HarperOne, 2014), 120.

15. Matthew 14:13–21; 15:32–39.

16. Emilie Schindler with Erika Rosenberg, *Where Light and Shadow Meet: A Memoir*, trans. Delores M. Koch (New York: W. W. Norton, 1997), ix.

When the war touched the Czech Republic, Oskar and Emilie were still newly married. Emilie notes that Hitler came to power amid turbulent times, yet she still could not imagine why anyone would blindly follow such a cruel man. "Of course, not every German was a Nazi. I know because I lived within that hell." She recalls Hitler's chilling words in the early days: "Whoever is with me will be able to live in a great Germany. . . . For those [against me] there will be no reprieve; there will be only winners." All pharaohs tend to sound alike, hungry for victory at the expense of others they deem a threat to their imagined greatness.

But Emilie confesses that in those early days she and Oskar became accomplices to what was happening. It began with Oskar joining a political group as a pragmatic move to get by without any trouble. It evolved into a job with the counterintelligence service, which Emilie, as a dutiful wife, sometimes assisted in. This is her regret—early complicity under this regime.

17. The factory recruited workers from the Plaschow camp. The rule was that everyone fourteen and older had to work. Those who were thirteen and younger were executed or used for medical experiments. The stakes were high for workers. Emilie notes that many parents misrepresented the age of their children just to keep them alive. She also said that Jewish women were scared to get pregnant—like Jochebed, they had much to fear for their children. Schindler, *Where Light and Shadow Meet*, 57.

18. Schindler, *Where Light and Shadow Meet*, 91.

19. Proverbs 31:30.

20. For an exploration of Jochebed as the archetype birth mother and the connection between injustice and relinquishment, especially in adoption, refer to my previous book, *Adopted*.

21. Nahum Sarna, *Exploring Exodus: The Origins of Biblical Israel* (New York: Schocken Books, 1996), 29.

22. The language used to describe Sarah's harsh treatment of Hagar, her slave, is the same language used to describe the harsh treatment of the Hebrews by their Egyptian masters. There is a reversal, and we are meant to hear that in the linguistic echoes between the two texts.

23. Phyllis Trible, "Ominous Beginnings for a Promise of Blessing," in *Hagar, Sarah, and Their Children: Jewish, Christian, and Muslim Perspectives*, ed. Phyllis Trible and Letty M. Russell (Louisville: Westminster John Knox, 2006), 48.

24. Genesis 21:16.

25. Patricia Nombuyiselo Noah's story is wonderfully told by her son, Trevor Noah, in *Born a Crime: Stories from a South African Childhood* (New York: Spiegl & Grau, 2016).

26. Brueggemann, "The Book of Exodus," 701.

CHAPTER 4

1. The name of Pharaoh's daughter is not mentioned in the Hebrew Bible. However, Jewish tradition offers different names for her. I follow Va-

yikra (Leviticus) Rabbah 1:3 when I call her Bithiah, Hebrew for "daughter of YHWH."

2. This narrative retelling of mine was previously published by *SheLoves Magazine* as "On the Shore of the Great River," February 10, 2015, https://she lovesmagazine.com/2015/shore-of-the-great-river/.

3. The infamous photograph of young Alan Kurdi was taken on September 2, 2015, by Nilüfer Demir.

4. See the Bereshit (Genesis) Rabbah, cited in Phyllis Trible, "Ominous Beginnings for a Promise of Blessing," and Adele Reinhartz and Miriam-Simma Walfish, "Conflict and Coexistence in Jewish Interpretation," both in *Hagar, Sarah, and Their Children: Jewish, Christian, and Muslim Perspectives*, ed. Phyllis Trible and Letty M. Russell (Louisville: Westminster John Knox, 2006), 64, 106, respectively.

5. Trible, "Ominous Beginnings," 37.

6. Islamic memory has Hajar, as they know her, running from Safa to Marwa desperately looking for help. Eventually the angel Gabriel comes to assist her and her son, guiding them to the waters of Zam-Zam. Riffat Hassan, "Islamic Hagar and Her Family," in Trible and Letty, *Hagar, Sarah, and Their Children*, 154.

7. "As for Ishmael, I have heard you. Behold, I will bless him and I will make him fruitful; and I will increase him in the much of muchness. Twelve princes he will father; and I will make him into a great nation." Genesis 17:20, translated from the Hebrew by Phyllis Trible, "Ominous Beginnings," 56.

8. It is also noteworthy that Hagar is the only woman in the Hebrew Bible who secures a wife for her son. This is typically the job of men, of fathers, in a patriarchal society. In doing so, Hagar becomes "a matriarch on par with the patriarch," in the words of Debbie Blue. *Consider the Women: A Provocative Guide to Three Matriarchs of the Bible* (Grand Rapids: Eerdmans, 2019), 41.

9. In her stunning poem "Hajar's Ram," Mohja Kahf explores how Sarah sacrificed Hagar, for whom there was no salvific ram. Read this and other poetic explorations of Hagar in Mohja Kahf, *Hagar Poems* (Fayetteville: University of Arkansas Press, 2016), 18. (I am indebted to John Noble for recommending this collection to me based on generous exchanges we had about Hagar and Exodus.)

10. Indeed, the text says that the actions of Pharaoh's daughter mirrored those of Levi's daughter. Both women saw-saw-took in short order, both taking maternal action on behalf of the boy. Jochebed saw he was good, saw she could not hide him any longer, and took him to the river. Bithiah saw the raft, saw the child, and took pity on him. Both mothered this baby boy. U. Cassuto, *A Commentary on the Book of Exodus* (Jerusalem: The Hebrew University Magnes Press, 1967), 19.

11. Ezekiel 29:3.

12. Christena Cleveland, "Jesus the Privileged" (blog post), September 23, 2013, www.christenacleveland.com/blogarchive/2013/09/jesus-the-privileged.

13. Exodus 1:22 ESV.

14. This brings the total mentions of *daughter* in this pericope to seven, a significant number in Hebrew literature. We are meant to notice the steady stream of daughters parading through this text. See Cassuto, *Commentary on Exodus*, 17.

15. Walter Brueggemann, "The Book of Exodus," in *The New Interpreter's Bible: A Commentary in Twelve Volumes*, vol. 1 (Nashville: Abingdon, 1994), 701.

16. Isaiah 40:31.

CHAPTER 5

1. See Shemot (Exodus) Rabbah 1:17 and M. Megillah 14a, among other midrash, as cited in Avivah Gottlieb Zornberg, *The Particulars of Rapture: Reflections on Exodus* (New York: Schocken Books, 2001), 68–70.

2. B. Megillah 14a, cited in Zornberg, *Particulars of Rapture*, 70.

3. The chant that went viral was "We call B. S." The intent was not to be crass but to allow those four simple syllables to move people to chant along.

4. Isaiah 11:1-6.

5. Luke 18:16-17.

6. Exodus 2:9.

7. See Jacqueline E. Lapsley, *Whispering the Word: Hearing Women's Stories in the Old Testament* (Louisville: Westminster John Knox, 2005), 69–88. This chapter, "Saving Women: Transgressive Values of Deliverance in Exodus 1-4," is succinct exegesis and insightful commentary on how the women crossed ethnic and socioeconomic barriers in this liberation narrative.

8. In his exegesis of Isaiah 11, Walter Brueggemann comments on the power of the *ruah*, or wind, at work in Exodus, with David, and with Jesus. Brueggemann, *Using God's Resources Wisely: Isaiah and Urban Possibility* (Louisville: Westminster John Knox, 1993), 19.

9. I first learned about skunk water in a refugee camp on the edge of Bethlehem called Aida. The IDF created skunk water as a form of crowd control aimed squarely at managing the Palestinian people. It is water infused with putrid agents that smell like rotting meat, decomposing bodies, and things much more pungent than a mere skunk. It is often blasted from water cannons, soaking streets, homes, clothes, and skin. The odor is inescapable and lingers for days, despite attempts to scrub it away. The IDF has weaponized water, which seems a particular cruelty since most Palestinian com-

munities live with limited access to potable water. While created for crowd control, it is used almost daily in Aida as a form of collective punishment. Israel has marketed skunk water to other police departments, including in the United States. It is reported that the St. Louis Metropolitan Police Department has purchased skunk water—so this might be hitting close to home sometime soon.

10. A bare-handed slap going up against an automatic rifle is akin to the rocks that were thrown against the IDF tanks rolling through the West Bank during the first intifada. It is a modern David and Goliath scenario that plays out time and time again under oppressive regimes.

11. Why is it that women and their hair always get our attention—be it Ahed Tamimi's long blond hair or the buzz cut of Emma González?

12. Ahed served eight months in prison for the slap—so did her mother. In the lifespan of a teenager, eight months is an eternity, yet it was her sacrifice for justice. On July 29, 2018, the day of her release, Ahed told crowds, "My happiness is not complete without my sisters, who are not with me." She was referring to the Palestinian female prisoners who still remain in captivity. Jaclynn Ashly, "Palestinian Teen Activist Ahed Tamimi Freed from Jail," Al Jazeera, July 29, 2018, https://www.aljazeera.com/news/2018/07/palestinian -ahed-tamimi-freed-jail-180729051621393.html.

13. It would be worthwhile to explore the work of Greta Thunberg, Isra Hirsi, and Autumn Peltier, young women advocating for climate change action.

CHAPTER 6

1. Exodus 2:10: "When the child grew up, [Jochebed] brought him to Pharaoh's daughter, and [Bithiah] took him as her son. [Bithiah] named him Moses, 'because,' she said, '[we] drew him out of the water.'"

2. In Egyptian tradition, the name Mose was usually combined with the name of a pharaoh or a god. So we see Ahmose (the son of or child of the moon), Ptahmose (maybe the son of a craftsman or maker), Ramose (the son of Ra, the sun god), and Thotmose (son of Thoth). But Bithiah, according to the narrator, chooses only Mose to refer to her son. She attaches no Egyptian man or god, not even her father the pharaoh, to the name of her adopted child.

3. These transliterations used by Walter Brueggemann help us see the similarity between the Egyptian name and the Hebrew name. Brueggemann, "The Book of Exodus," in *The New Interpreter's Bible: A Commentary in Twelve Volumes*, vol. 1 (Nashville: Abingdon, 1994), 699.

4. Commentators note that the Egyptian *Mose* and the Hebrew *Masa* are

homonyms. But U. Cassuto comments that while Bithiah explains that Masa means "the one drawn out," indicating that she drew the child out of the water, the form of Masa in the text actually means "he who draws out," suggesting that "this child was destined to be 'the deliverer of his people' from the sea of servitude"—in other words, that Moses is the actor rather than the one acted upon. Cassuto, *A Commentary on the Book of Exodus* (Jerusalem: The Hebrew University Magnes Press, 1967), 20–21.

5. The dynamics around naming were similar in ancient Egypt, where the high infant mortality rate meant delayed naming. Nahum Sarna, *Exodus, The JPS Torah Commentary* (Philadelphia: Jewish Publication Society, 1991), 10; *Exploring Exodus* (New York: Schocken Books, 1996), 32.

6. Missionaries in Burundi instructed all Burundian converts to change their names, and those of their children, to European names. The reason? The missionaries could pronounce the European names. But the new names held no prophetic meaning or promise like their Kirundi names. It is a sad part of the missionary legacy in the region.

7. I'm grateful to my friend Elie Pritz for sharing some of her knowledge of Hebrew. *Tinoki* is "little baby," specific to a boy, and *matoki* means "sweet thing" and often functions as a term of endearment. I imagine these might have been nicknames for the young baby before he was named by Bithiah.

8. Sarah Bessey, "In Which I Am Learning to Live with the Ache" (blog post), January 20, 2014, https://sarahbessey.com/learning-live-ache/; "Off Brand" (blog post), May 4, 2016, https://sarahbessey.com/off-brand/.

9. I think of Lamentations, the five poems that Walter Brueggemann calls the grief work of the Old Testament. Daughter Zion cries out in the aftermath of Jerusalem's destruction. She has lost everything, even her children. She hurls graphic images and cries hot tears. She seethes with sorrow. Did Jochebed sink into songs of sadness after she made that final Nile crossing? I imagine lullabies that became lamentations, bearing witness to the truth that many liberation songs are shaped by loss.

10. The dual nature of his name points to his membership in two communities. Carol Meyers, *Exodus* (Cambridge: Cambridge University Press, 2005), 44.

11. John Paul Lederach and Angela Jill Lederach, *When Blood and Bones Cry Out: Journeys through the Soundscape of Healing and Reconciliation* (Oxford: Oxford University Press, 2010).

12. Lederach and Lederach, *When Blood and Bones Cry Out*, 148.

13. Not every adoption is an act of justice. We are learning more about unethical adoptions that enmesh us in the complicated realities of supply and demand, sometimes with overtones of colonization and our own savior complexes. We also must be honest about adoption as a tool of injustice, as in the Sixties Scoop in Canada, where Indigenous children were removed from their

homes and put up for adoption with the intent of separating them from their culture. White families eligible to adopt were told that the children were willingly relinquished and often didn't realize they were participating in a deep act of injustice against the Indigenous community, but the injustice remains.

14. Lederach and Lederach, *When Blood and Bones Cry Out*, 160–66.

15. Lederach and Lederach, *When Blood and Bones Cry Out*, 158.

16. Luke 1:26-38 tells of Gabriel's annunciation to Mary, and Luke 1:39-56 tells of Mary's visit to Elizabeth.

17. Did this make Mary think of the midwives, Shiphrah and Puah, who received God's favor after defying Pharaoh's order to kill baby boys at birth? Did it make her wonder if she was receiving the word of favor as a foretelling—that she would need to defy Caesar, the pharaoh of her day, to raise her son?

18. "Isaiah and the Mission of the Church" was preached by Walter Brueggemann at Mars Hill Church in Grand Rapids, Michigan, in July 2008.

CHAPTER 7

1. This is how the Qur'an speaks of Moses's arrival at adulthood (Al-Qasas 28:14). The text contains what many read as a reference to both his physical growth and his intellectual or psychological growth.

2. Exodus 2:11.

3. For a more thorough exploration of my thoughts on adoptees and questions about family/countries/cultures of origin, refer to my chapter on return in *Adopted: The Sacrament of Belonging in a Fractured World* (Grand Rapids: Eerdmans, 2017).

4. Exodus 2:12.

5. Genesis 24:11; 29:2.

6. Robert Alter, *The Art of Biblical Narrative* (New York: Basic Books, 1983), 50–58.

7. Nahum Sarna, *The JPS Torah Commentary: Exodus* (Philadelphia: Jewish Publication Society, 1991), 12.

8. Later in Exodus he will be called Jethro. This has made some wonder if Reuel is actually the grandfather of the daughters. But tradition seems to prefer Jethro as his name, the priest of Midian and father to seven daughters.

9. Psalm 23 and John 10:1-18 give us pictures of what good shepherds looked like in the ancient Near East.

10. Amahoro Africa is a conversation founded and hosted by Claude and me. We gather African leaders, both thinkers and practitioners, to consider African challenges and converse together about possible solutions.

11. To read Idelette's summary of the identity card initiative, see "Bubanza

Project: Can Love Move This Mountain in Burundi?," *SheLoves Magazine*, January 31, 2012, http://shelovesmagazine.com/2012/sheloves-bubanza-project-can -love-move-this-mountain-in-burundi/. These are her words about that day in Bubanza among the women: "Bubanza: We Danced on Holy Ground," *SheLoves Magazine*, June 12, 2012, https://shelovesmagazine.com/2012/bubanza-we -danced-on-holy-ground/.

12. Parts of this story were previously published in "Hidden Identity," *SheLoves Magazine*, February 5, 2018, https://shelovesmagazine.com/2018 /hidden-identity/.

13. Ada María Isasi-Díaz, *Mujerista Theology* (Maryknoll, NY: Orbis Books, 1996), 22. Her entire work is recommended, but for more on solidarity, read chapter 5 in full.

14. Tamim Al-Barghouti, *In Jerusalem and Other Poems, 1997–2017* (Northampton, MA: Interlink Books, 2017), 65–66.

CHAPTER 8

1. Exodus 2:21–22.

2. A portion of this section first appeared in "ShePonders: Another Anointing," *SheLoves Magazine*, November 15, 2011, https://shelovesmagazine .com/2011/sheponders-another-anointing/.

3. Richard A. Horsley says that when the woman anointed Jesus, she was "literally 'messiah-ing' or 'christ-ing' him." Horsley, *Hearing the Whole Story: The Politics of Plot in Mark's Gospel* (Louisville: Westminster John Knox, 2001), 207.

4. Emmanuel Katongole is a professor at Notre Dame University and a Catholic priest. His books include *A Mirror to the Church: Resurrecting Faith after the Genocide in Rwanda* (Grand Rapids: Zondervan, 2009); *Reconciling All Things: A Christian Vision for Justice, Peace, and Reconciliation* (Downers Grove, IL: IVP Books, 2008); and *Born from Lament: The Theology and Politics of Hope in Africa* (Grand Rapids: Eerdmans, 2017).

5. Proverbs 31:10, 18.

6. Carol Meyers has written extensively on the work of women in ancient Israel and parses a more nuanced understanding of patriarchy in *Discovering Eve: Ancient Israelite Women in Context* (New York: Oxford University Press, 1988), 24–46.

7. Carol Meyers speaks to the "technical behaviors" and "specialized knowledge" that women passed down and practiced in what she calls "informal household religious culture." Meyers, *Households and Holiness: The Religious Culture of Israelite Women* (Philadelphia: Fortress, 2005), 61.

8. In Genesis 30:14–17, Reuben grows (or harvests) mandrakes, known

for their fertility-enhancing properties. Rachel, still barren, begs Leah for her son's mandrakes. But Leah denies her—a cold retribution for Rachel having stolen the affections of their husband, Jacob.

9. Meyers, *Households and Holiness*, 41.

10. See Meyers, *Households and Holiness*, 7, for men and women in religious practices; 11, for women overseeing household practice; and 42–43, for women performing circumcisions.

11. I offered *amahoro*, a Bantu word meaning "peace" or "shalom" that is a traditional greeting in Burundi. Idelette spoke of *ubuntu*, a word from South Africa that signifies interconnection and solidarity.

12. Exodus 4:24–26.

13. This is all the more fascinating when we consider Zipporah's actions in contrast to Moses's response to God's call. Moses resists the initial call, believing he is not worthy—that he can't speak straight or command the attention of Pharaoh. Where Moses is conflicted and riddled with hesitation, Zipporah is decisive and discerning without any delay.

14. A portion of this section originally appeared in "ShePonders: Salvation Oracles," *SheLoves Magazine*, October 16, 2012, https://shelovesmag azine.com/2012/sheponders-salvation-oracles/.

CHAPTER 9

1. Nahum Sarna, *Exploring Exodus: The Origins of Biblical Israel* (New York: Schocken Books, 1996), 21.

2. I love that John Lewis has given us the phrase "good trouble." It describes so well the work of justice that upends the status quo, that appears to be trouble but demands justice for the common good. It applies to the current era in the United States but is also apropos for the troubled days in Egypt.

3. For further exploration of Naomi's predicament, read *Who Are You, My Daughter? Reading Ruth Through Image and Text* by Ellen F. Davis and Margaret Adams Parker (Louisville: Westminster John Knox, 2003) and *Finding God in the Margins: The Book of Ruth* by Carolyn Custis James (Bellingham, WA: Lexham, 2018). The latter work offers thoughtful connections on the contemporaneity of Naomi and Ruth's story.

4. Carol Meyers, "Women of Bethlehem," in *Women in Scripture: A Dictionary of Named and Unnamed Women in the Hebrew Bible, the Apocryphal/Deuterocanonical Books, and the New Testament*, ed. Carol Meyers (Grand Rapids: Eerdmans, 2000), 253.

5. In the book of Ruth, we see the women of Bethlehem in 1:19 and 4:14–15 and then the women of the neighborhood in 4:17. They are distinct in the text, yet I believe that, together, they point to the network of neighborly women

in general and how they operate. For more detailed commentary, see Meyers, "Women of Bethlehem," in *Women in Scripture*, 253.

6. "The existence of such women's networks is thus barely visible in the Hebrew Bible, though other terms (such as 'companions' in Judges 11:37-38) may signify a related instance of extra-familial female bonding." Meyers, "Women of the Neighborhood," in *Women in Scripture*, 254.

7. The feminine noun for *neighbors* is used in Exodus 3:22 and Ruth 4:17. Meyers, "Women of the Neighborhood," 254.

8. In Exodus 3:21-22 and again in Exodus 11:2-3, we see the presence of gender-based networks. Carol Meyers comments: "Men and women apparently have gender-specific networks with their 'neighbors' that allow them to request valuable items." This will come into play more fully as we explore the giving and taking of items between neighbors. Meyers, "Women (and Men) with Jewelry and Clothing," in *Women in Scripture*, 188.

9. Exodus 3:21-22.

10. Genesis 15:13-14.

11. We can see congruence with Deuteronomy 15:14, where the Mosaic law commands slaves to be emancipated with economic means (from the flock, the threshing floor, the winepress) to start their life of freedom. They are not to leave "empty-handed."

12. Exodus 3:21-22.

13. Exodus 11:2-3.

14. Exodus 12:33-36.

15. Dalia Landau's story can be found in the compelling book *The Lemon Tree: An Arab, a Jew, and the Heart of the Middle East* by Sandy Tolan (New York: Bloomsbury, 2006). You might also check out the Peace Heroes curriculum, developed by Elie Pritz to teach students history through the lens of peacemakers, at www.globalpeaceheroes.org.

16. Pritz, unpublished unit on Dalia Landau, 14.

17. Jubilee, or the year of release, is an economic practice prescribed in Deuteronomy 15 and Leviticus 25 and alluded to in Isaiah 61. Every fiftieth year the shofar is to sound and a major recalibration of the economy happens: slaves are set free, debts are forgiven, and land is returned to original owners who lost it in the rough-and-tumble of the economy. This practice meant that no family was locked in poverty permanently; everyone got a chance to begin again when the horn blew. Jesus mentions the year of release in his inaugural speech in a local synagogue, saying, through his reading of the Isaiah scroll, that he will put Jubilee into motion (Luke 4:14-21).

18. Tolan, *The Lemon Tree*, 247.

19. Did the Israelites really battle the enemy? It seems they prayed and praised and God set an ambush, resulting in the other warring forces fighting one another. Jehoshaphat and his soldiers arrived to the sight of corpses

and treasures strewn about the battlefield. So they killed no one, according to the Chronicler (2 Chron. 20:20-25). This sounds like the victor's version of history. Most likely the Israelite army had a hand in the bloody incident, which left no one alive to offer a counternarrative.

20. See note 17 above.

21. Nahum Sarna defines *plunder* in this text as "stripping" and points to the literal use of the word in 2 Chronicles 20:25. But he believes that in this text, *plunder* functions as hyperbole. Sarna, *The JPS Torah Commentary: Exodus* (Philadelphia: Jewish Publication Society, 1991), 19.

22. Walter Brueggemann discusses this dynamic as he interacts with David Daube's *The Exodus Pattern in the Bible* (London: Faber and Faber, 1963), 55-61. However, Brueggemann seems to see this text as a bit of "palpable fiction." He goes on to say that the Exodus text isn't about realism regarding plunder. This is a story meant to light our theological imagination. He notes the similarity between Exodus 12:35-36 and Isaiah 40, where there is no rush required when returning to Jerusalem from Babylonian captivity. Imagine departing Babylon at your leisure, then imagine taking what you need as you leave Egypt. Brueggemann, "The Book of Exodus," in *The New Interpreter's Bible: A Commentary in Twelve Volumes*, vol. 1 (Nashville: Abingdon, 1994), 770.

23. Ta-Nehisi Coates writes about the incalculable number and overwhelming logistics often shutting down our national curiosity in his *Atlantic* article "The Case for Reparations." This can also be found in his book *We Were Eight Years in Power: An American Tragedy* (New York: One World, 2017), 151-208.

CHAPTER 10

1. Sea of Reeds, *yam suf* in Hebrew, has generally been translated "Red Sea" in English Bibles until recently. See Nahum Sarna, *Exploring Exodus: The Origins of Biblical Israel* (New York: Schocken Books, 1996), 103-7.

2. The dramatic covenant-cutting ceremony is first described in Genesis 15: animals were split in two and "a smoking fire pot with a flaming torch passed between these pieces" (v. 17). In this same passage Abraham learns of a future enslavement in Egypt for his progeny that will nonetheless culminate in an emancipatory departure laden with possessions (vv. 13-14).

3. There is a rabbinic tradition that says that when the Egyptians died at sea in the wake of the exodus, God silenced the angels from singing. "How dare you sing for joy when my creatures are dying" (Talmud, Megillah 10b).

4. For more on the scholarship that points to Miriam as the original author of the Song of the Sea (Exod. 15:1-21), see Carol Meyers, *Exodus* (Cambridge: Cambridge University Press, 2005), 116, and Wilda C. Gafney,

Womanist Midrash: A Reintroduction to the Women of the Torah and the Throne (Louisville: Westminster John Knox, 2017), 98.

5. "The instrument mentioned in Exodus 15:20 is probably a hand-drum, a small hand-held frame drum anachronistically translated 'tambourine' in many English versions. It happens to be the only percussion instrument mentioned in the Hebrew Bible; and in every case in which the gender of musicians is stipulated, women are the drummers." Meyers, *Exodus*, 116.

6. Not only this, but Miriam was the only prophet in Egypt for a long time. Gafney, *Womanist Midrash*, 95.

7. Meyers, *Exodus*, 116, 119.

8. Ivone Gebara and Maria Clara Bingemer, *Mary: Mother of God, Mother of the Poor* (Maryknoll, NY: Orbis Books, 1996), 47.

9. Miriam was a common name in the New Testament era, and "all the Marys in the NT—six or seven, depending on how one counts—are Miriams." Gafney, *Womanist Midrash*, 96.

10. While technically unknown, some church traditions name Joachim and Anne as the parents of Mary.

11. Translation: "Yes, we can" or "Yes, it is possible."

12. *Dolores*, directed by Peter Bratt (2017; Arlington, VA: PBS, 2018), DVD. Dolores Huerta is an amazing Mexican American labor leader and activist, and her story should be more widely known. I recommend this documentary, produced by Carlos Santana.

13. In 2010, for example, the Texas Board of Education removed Dolores Huerta from the state's elementary school curriculum, and Arizona lawmakers passed a ban (struck down in 2017) on ethnic studies classes in public schools, specifically targeting the Tucson United School District's Mexican American studies program. The occasional banning of Dolores's story reminds me of the similarly mixed reception of Mary's Magnificat, banned in India, Guatemala, and Argentina at various times in history. (See D. L. Mayfield, "Mary's 'Magnificat' in the Bible Is Revolutionary. Some Evangelicals Silence Her," *Washington Post*, December 20, 2018, https://www.washingtonpost.com/religion/2018/12/20/marys -magnificat-bible-is-revolutionary-so-evangelicals-silence-it/.)